WORLD CLASS COACHING

Training Sessions of English Premier League Teams
(Plus Other British Teams and Academies)

Edited by

Mike Saif

Published by
WORLD CLASS COACHING

First published December, 2005 by
WORLD CLASS COACHING 15004 Buena Vista Drive, Leawood, KS 66224 (913) 402-0030

ISBN 0-9773419-0-9

Material in this book was originally published as magazines in the USA and UK

Edited by Mike Saif

Cover by John Babcock, Illustration & Design

Published by

WORLD CLASS COACHING

WORLD CLASS COACHING

Training Sessions of English Premier League Teams

(Plus Other British Teams and Academies)

01	Opposing Player	→	Path of Player	〜→	Path of Dribble
X1	4-4-2 Player	⇢	Path of Ball	⬭	Target Area

Introduction

Training Sessions of English Premier League Teams (Plus Other British Teams and Academies) is taken from material first published in the 2004 and 2005 issues of the WORLD CLASS COACHING magazine.

The WORLD CLASS COACHING magazine is the only publication in the world that publishes the training sessions of the world's top teams and coaches. It is regarded as the authoritative publication of choice for soccer coaches worldwide with thousands of coaches from over 60 countries subscribing to this bi-monthly magazine.

In this book are sessions from English Premier League teams and their Academies like Manchester United, Liverpool, Everton and Fulham. Also included are sessions from England National Teams, and top British clubs like Glasgow Rangers, Glasgow Celtic, Crystal Palace, Leeds United, Norwich City, Sheffield United. These, plus sessions from David Platt, Wayne Harrison, Derek Broadley, and conditioning sessions from world renowned Roger Spry make this book a must have for any serious soccer coach.

Topics include, Pressing as a Team, Defending With 3 or 4 Defenders, Crossing and Finishing, Working With a Back Four, Improving Team Shape, Small-Sided Games, Training Overlaps, Improving Speed of Play and many other sessions.

Each training session has detailed explanations and is accompanied with easy-to-read diagrams to make this book the perfect reference for any level of coach.

Linfield F.C - N. Ireland

Linfield Football Club was formed in 1886 in Belfast, Northern Ireland and is a club whose playing record is unsurpassed in Irish soccer having won the League Championship 44 times and represented Northern Ireland in European competition 71 times. Their Windsor Park Stadium is also the home of the National team. This session was conducted by first team coach Bryan McLoughlin, a UEFA B licence coach.

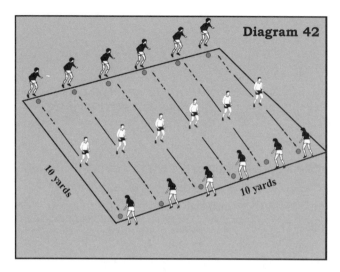

Diagram 42

10 yards

10 yards

Warm-Up

Eighteen players run in groups of three diagonally across the field, occasionally stopping for some static and dynamic stretches.

Technical Practice

Players are arranged in six groups of three. The two players on the outside have a ball each in their hands. The middle player runs to a player who serves the ball and receives a return pass. The middle player then turns sharply and runs to the other player opposite to do the same. Each player works for one minute on the same technique before he changes with a teammate. After the three players have completed the required technique, the coach then selects another technique/skill.

Techniques Covered:

• Instep volley
• Volley with the outside of the foot
• Control the ball using the thigh before a volley return
• Control with the chest before a half volley return
• Jump to head the ball to the server's feet
• Servers choice - a mixture of all of the above

Coaching Points

• Good first touch, open body shape
• Firm contact with the ball
• Control the ball by withdrawing surface
• Concentrate on the ball before the turn

Agility

This drill works on the player's agility. Using two identical setups allows four players to run simultaneously. The players are timed by the coach, who identifies the winners. Players must take care when crossing paths.

Sequence

• A to B: Sprint forwards
• B to C: Lateral (sideways) skip
• C to D: Sprint forwards
• D to E: Sprint backwards
• E to F: Sideways - fast foot cones or ladders can be used
• F to G: Sprint forwards
• G to H: Sprint forwards

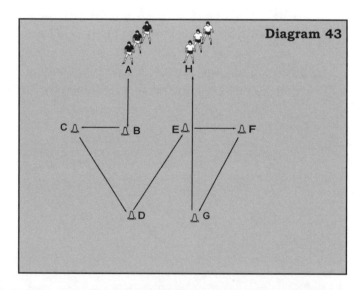

Diagram 43

Linfield F.C - N. Ireland

Technique

Each of the three groups of six players work in a 20 x 20-yard area on passing and control under pressure. Each player in each corner has a ball. The attacker demands the ball from any corner player, the defender applies pressure to intercept the pass. The attacker must take two touches, therefore shielding the ball before returning it and demanding another pass from a different corner. These two players work for one minute and then change with any corner pairing. And so the sequence continues.

Progression

Two balls are then removed from each group. Now the attacker demands a ball and must play it to one of the open corner players. The attacker now has unlimited touches.

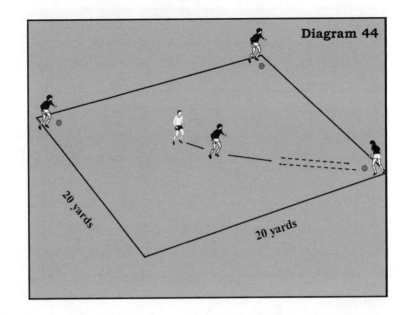

Diagram 44

20 yards

20 yards

Progression

The last progression is a 4 v 2 keep-away situation for one minute with only two corners available to play passes to.

Functional Play

The next drill is a defense versus attack practice focusing on finishing under pressure. The players are divided into three teams of six. The teams take turns to act as attackers, defenders and servers and each 'game' lasts six minutes. On the coach's command, a server starts the play by passing to the attacking team who attempts to score as many goals as possible in the time allotted. As soon as the ball goes out of the area, the coach instructs another server to pass a new ball to the attacking team. If the defenders gain possession, they try to keep the ball as long as possible to restrict the goalscoring opportunities for the attackers. The two wide servers, on the coaches command, must cross the ball to the attackers to attack.

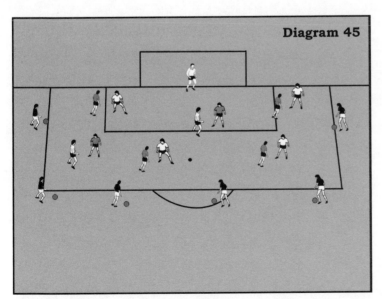

Diagram 45

Coaching Points

- Quality of cross from wide servers
- Good passing technique
- Shoot at first opportunity
- Do not over pass

If the goalkeeper makes a save, the ball can be thrown to the defending team to possess.

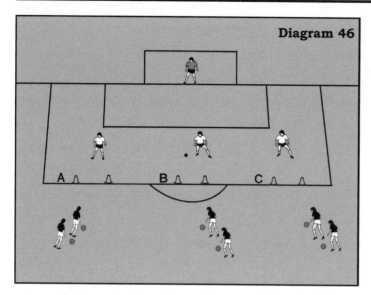

Diagram 46

Finishing and Defending: 1 v 1

The final drill focuses on finishing and defending in 1 v 1 situations. The coach calls the attacker in position 'A' to run through the two cones (1 yard apart) and 'take on' the defender. As soon as the attacker goes through the cones, the defender becomes 'live'. Play stops when a shot is taken, the defender wins the ball, or the ball goes out of play. The coach then calls one of the other two attackers to start. Players rotate positions.

Coaching Points

- Focus on attacking at speed
- Close ball control
- Accurate shooting
- Early shooting

Options

- If an attacker scores, he can continue as the attacker until he fails to score
- Every attempt is played to the finish, i.e. if a defender wins possession he can instantly try to score
- Limit the time to shoot

The session ends with a 10 minute cool down and stretch.

Conditioning With The Ball

This article is contributed by conditioning expert Roger Spry. Spry has worked with soccer teams worldwide, including F.C. Porto and Sporting Lisbon in Portugal, Aston Villa and Sheffield Wednesday in England and Vissel Kobe in Japan. Spry has also been a consultant to the Danish, Dutch, Austrian, Scottish, Welsh, Swedish, Norwegian, Japanese, Portuguese, American, and Georgian Football Associations. For more information visit www.eteamz.com/sites/fitness4soccer.

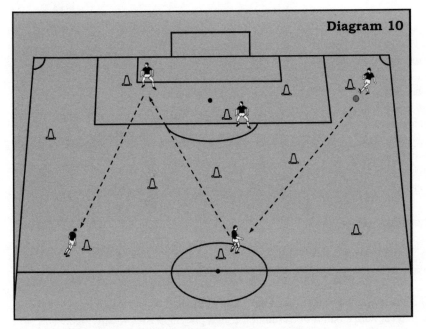

Diagram 10

Passing/Conditioning Drill

This is a great passing and awareness drill and can be used at all levels. This training drill was used extensively when I worked at F.C.Porto

1. Pass to any player and immediately sprint to an empty cone.
2. Pass to another player and all of the team must sprint to an empty cone.
3. Sprint with the ball to an empty cone, pass to any player, and then sprint to another empty cone.
4. Sprint with the ball to an empty cone, pass to another player, then all of the team must sprint to an empty cone.
5. Pass to another player, then all of the team must sprint backwards to an empty cone.
6. Pass to another player, sprint backwards to a cone, then sprint forwards to another cone.
7. Sprint with the ball to an empty cone, all of the players sprint to an empty cone, pass the ball and then everyone sprints to another empty cone.
8. Pass to an empty cone and the nearest player sprints to receive the ball, whilst all of the other players sprint sideways to an empty cone.

Using this set-up, a myriad of diverse movements and shapes can be worked on, only limited by the coaches or the players imagination.

These types of drills involve passing, running, decision-making, finding space, and can be used throughout the season, depending on what you require. For more endurance emphasis, do the drill on a full pitch; for pure speed and shorter explosive movements, an area the size of the penalty area is used.

Also, because of the design of the drill, position related training could be undertaken (shorter distances for the strikers, bigger areas and distances for the midfield for example).

This drill can be done very effectively indoors for extreme reactions. I have used this drill all over the world with excellent results. Remember, it is only limited by your imagination. It isn't enough to just work harder, you must "imagine harder" as well.

Linfield F.C, N. Ireland

Linfield Football Club was formed in 1886 in Belfast, Northern Ireland and is a club whose playing record is unsurpassed in Irish soccer having won the League Championship 44 times and represented Northern Ireland in European competition 71 times. Their Windsor Park Stadium is also the home of the National team. This session was conducted by first team coach Bryan McLoughlin, a UEFA B licence coach.

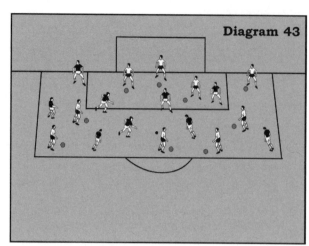

Diagram 43

Warm-Up

Eighteen players warm up via a mixture of jogging, half pace and three quarter pace running over half the length of the pitch followed by some static stretching. The players then use the 18-yard area to practice passing and control exercises with nine balls. The focus is on good first touch, body posture, accuracy and communication. The players work in pairs, moving freely, with unlimited touches. The players should be aware of the movement of other players in close proximity in terms of ball control. After five minutes, the players stop and continue with stretching exercises.

Several different control/passing drills are performed:

- Keep-away - One player keeps the ball away from the other.
- Keep-away and beat a player - Same as previous but now once a turn is achieved, the player tries to go past his opponent.
- Juggling and running - One player juggles the ball while the other runs at half pace to the half way line and back.
- With all the players in the 18-yard box, nine players with a ball move around the area playing passes to any 'open' player. The receiving player uses a one-touch to pass into space as the return pass.

Coaching Points
- Good communication
- Good first touch
- Good movement
- Good vision
- The quality weight of the pass

Progression

As above, but now instead of a return pass into space, the receiving player controls the ball, turns away and makes a pass to a new player. Each player is restricted to three touches and every player must keep moving.

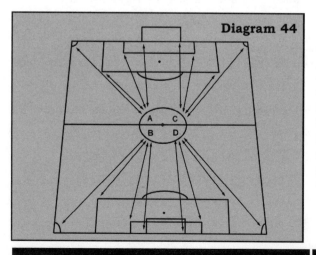

Diagram 44

Endurance Exercises

Sixteen players take part forming four teams of four for a relay race with the losing team performing a body exercise. Four teams: A, B, C & D run as a relay to the cones/points indicated by the coach. There are four separate races performed without the ball, then with the ball (focusing on good ball control running at speed). When using a ball, a pass is permitted when the returning player is inside the center circle.

Linfield F.C, N. Ireland

Functional Practice

This drill focuses on short and long passing under pressure. Eighteen players are divided into three teams of six, with each team in a different color and placed in three different zones/areas. Team A (black), in zone 1, start with a ball, and on the coach's command, three players from team B (grey team), from zone 2, try to win the ball. Team A needs to complete five short passes before the next player must make a long pass to Team C (white team) in zone 3. If they are successful, the other three players from the grey team go into zone 3 to try win the ball. The sequence continues until the chasing three players win possession or if the long pass goes out of the playing area. When this happens, the team that loses possession now goes into the central area (zone 2).

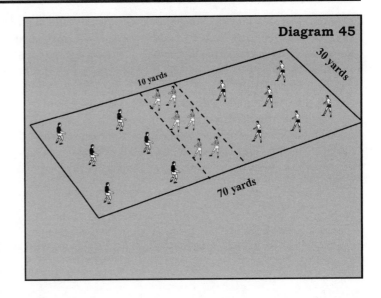

Diagram 45

Progression

To keep the session going at a high pace, the coach delivers new balls to keep the exercise from breaking down. The coach encourages the 'working team' to win possession as quickly as possible. This is a physically demanding exercise when played at a high tempo and it instills the principle of working as a unit, as well as enforcing accurate short and long passing. The session can be developed by restricting the number of touches in zones 1 and 3 or by enabling the ball to be intercepted as it goes through zone 2.

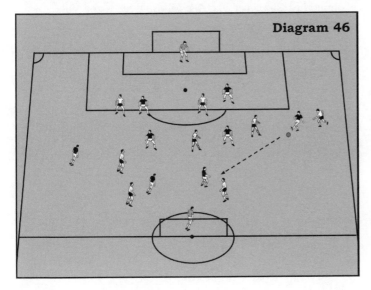

Diagram 46

Final Exercise

Play 8 v 8 with two goalkeepers using half a field working on quick counter-attacking with throws for the goalkeeper. A goal can only be scored from a cross ball or from a pass laid back to a player to shoot.

A 10-minute cool down jog and stretch ends the session.

Golden Goal

This goal was scored by Lee Chapman against Aston Villa in an English Premier League game during Leeds United's 1991/92 Championship season. A long overlap run by the fullback is largely responsible. Only the players involved are shown so as not to clutter the diagram.

Gordon Strachan receives the ball just inside his own half on the right flank. He has space in front of him and attacks it with a penetrating run inside toward the goal. As Strachan receives the ball, Mel Sterland, who was known for his raiding runs down the right flank, starts his overlapping run from inside his own half.

As Strachan approaches the penalty area, the defender who is covering Sterland's run has no option but to move inside to stop Strachan. At this point, Strachan plays the ball out wide to an unmarked Sterland.

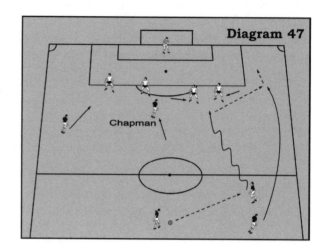

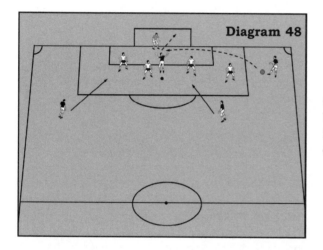

On receiving the ball, Sterland takes one touch to push the ball out of his feet and then delivers a perfect cross for the incoming Lee Chapman who soars above three Aston Villa defenders.

Conditioning With The Ball

This article is contributed by conditioning expert Roger Spry. Spry has worked with soccer teams worldwide, including F.C. Porto and Sporting Lisbon in Portugal, Aston Villa and Sheffield Wednesday in England and Vissel Kobe in Japan. Spry has also been a consultant to the Danish, Dutch, Austrian, Scottish, Welsh, Swedish, Norwegian, Japanese, Portuguese, American, and Georgian Football Associations. For more information visit www.eteamz.com/sites/ fitness4soccer.

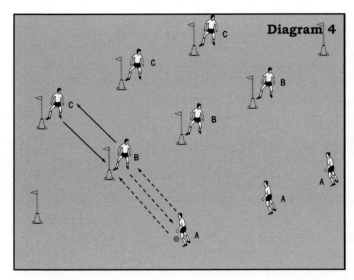

Diagram 4

Passing and Pattern Runs

These drills are to practice quality passing and movement toward and away from the ball.

Player A passes a straight ball to player B, who passes back to player A. After B has played the ball, he then runs backward to position C. At the same time, player C sprints forward to position B and receives the next pass. Player A continues passing without waiting for either of the players, passing to a zone and not a player.

Variation

Player A passes a straight pass to player at B, who passes back to player A. After B has played the ball he turns, and sprints forward to position C. At the same time player C sprints forward to position B and receives the next pass. Player A continues passing without waiting.

Variation

Player A passes a straight pass to player at B, who passes back to player A. After B has played the ball, he runs sideways to the next pole on the left, sprints backward to position C, and then sprints forward to position B. At the same time, player C sprints forwards to position B and receives the next pass. Player A continues without waiting for either of the players, he passes to a zone not a player.

Variation

Player A passes a straight pass to player at B, who passes back to player A. After B has played the ball, he runs sideways to the next pole on the left, turns and sprints forward to position C, and then sprints forward to position B. At the same time, player C sprints forward to position B and receives the next pass. Player A continues passing without waiting.

Variation

Player A passes a straight pass to player at B, who passes back to player A. After B has played the ball, he runs sideways to the next pole on the right, sprints backward to position C, and then sprints forward to position B. At the same time, player C sprints forward to position B and receives the next pass. Player A continues passing without waiting.

Variation

Player A passes a straight pass to player at B, who passes back to player A. After B has played the ball, he runs sideways to the next pole on the right, sprints forward to position C, and then sprints forwards to position B. At the same time player C sprints forward to position B and receives the next pass. Player A continues passing without waiting.

This drill can be done in a variety of ways:
- Vary the distance between the poles to give an all around passing and sprinting effect
- Work for one minute in each position and then change
- Use either one-touch passing, or if the players conditioning is not up to it, the player in position A can decide to have more touches (good exercise for decision making)

Conditioning With The Ball

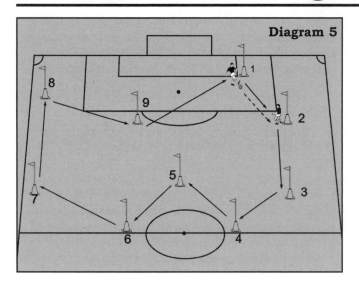

Diagram 5

Passing and Communication Drill

Working in pairs, one player is on pole 1 and his partner on pole 2. Player on pole 1 passes to player on pole 2 and sprints after his own pass, player on pole 2 stops the ball and sprints off to pole 3, and so on around the circuit until both players arrive at the starting pole. The players change positions and roles and repeat.

Variation

Working in pairs, one player is on pole 1 and his partner on pole 2. Player on pole 1 passes to player on pole 2 and sprints after his own pass, player on pole 2 lays the ball off to one side of pole 2 and sprints off to the next pole, and so on around the circuit.

Variation

Working in pairs, one player is on pole 1 and his partner on pole 2. Player on pole 1 sprints with the ball to pole 2, at the same time player on pole 2 sprints to pole 3. The first player then passes to the second player and sprints after his own pass, the second player stops the ball and sprints off to pole 4, and so on around the circuit.

Variation

Working in pairs, one player is on pole 1 and his partner on pole 2. Player on pole 1 sprints with the ball to pole 2, at the same time player on pole 2 sprints to pole 3. The first player then passes to the second player and sprints after his pass, the second player lays the ball off to one side of the pole and sprints off to pole 4, and so on around the circuit.

This drill can be done in a variety of ways:
• Vary the distance between the poles to give an all around passing and sprinting effect
• Use the whole field to increase the training load, towards endurance
• Use only the penalty area to increase the demands toward explosive short passing movement and reception

Physical Fitness Activity

To prepare the players to perform physically and mentally to their optimum levels, set up a grid within a grid. The size is dependant on the physical condition of your players. All of the players start within the inner grid. In the outer grid put hurdles, medicine balls, poles, slalom courses or whatever equipment you have at hand. The players are numbered 1 through 10 (or however many players you have). Player number one passes to number two, number two to number three and so on until the last player plays a pass back to number one.

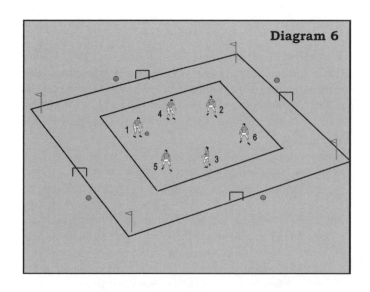

Diagram 6

This drill can be done in a variety of ways:
• From hand to hand
• From foot to foot on the floor one touch
• One touch, left foot only
• One touch, right foot only

Conditioning With The Ball

Variations

As soon as a player has passed the ball, he must then undertake a task before he can rejoin the inner grid again:

- Sprint and touch any pole on the outer grid
- Sprint and jump over any hurdle on the outer grid
- Sprint to the outer grid and with any ball, juggle for 20 touches

Progressions

Players go unnumbered, the player who calls for the ball receives the pass and then must undertake a task before he can rejoin the inner grid:

- Sprint and touch any two poles on the outer grid
- Sprint and jump over any hurdle and touch a pole on the outer grid
- Sprint to the outer grid and with any ball, juggle for 20 touches and then jump over two different hurdles

Variation

Players are numbered. Player number one passes to number two, number two to number three and so on until the last player plays a pass back to number one, but this time there are two balls going around the grid (the only rule is that the balls never touch):

This drill can be done in a variety of ways:

- From hand to hand
- From foot to foot on the floor one touch
- One touch, left foot only
- One touch, right foot only

As soon as the player passes the ball, he must undertake a task before he can rejoin the inner grid again.

Variation

Players go unnumbered, again with two balls going around the grid (balls are not allowed to touch) . The player who calls for the ball, receives the pass and then sprints and touches any two different poles on the outer grid:

- Sprint and jump over any hurdle and touch a pole on the outer grid
- Sprint to the outer grid and with any ball, juggle for 20 touches and then jump over two different hurdles

Golden Goal

This goal was scored by Paul Scholes of Manchester United in an English Premier League game against Southampton on January 31, 2004. The build up starts with a throw-in just in the attacking half. Three one-touch volley passes and two one-touch shots later (all in the space of about 6 seconds), a goal of immense quality is scored.

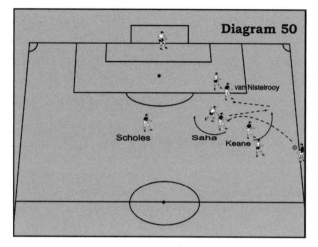

Diagram 50

The throw-in is taken just inside the attacking half. The ball is thrown over the head of Roy Keane for Louis Saha, who chests the ball down for Keane, who had quickly turned as the ball went over his head.

Keane takes the ball out of the air and plays it with one touch to Ruud van Nistelrooy.

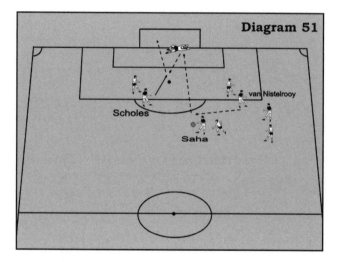

Diagram 51

Van Nistelrooy flicks the ball with the outside of his right foot into the path of Saha, who had turned and made his run after chesting the ball to Keane.

Saha shoots with his first touch, with his left foot from 25 yards. The Southampton goalkeeper makes the save but is unable to hold onto the ball.

Paul Scholes, who has been waiting around the edge of the penalty area, follows the shot from Saha and pounces on the rebound to score a memorable goal.

Cambridge United U13's

These two sessions are contributed by Martyn Pert, a UEFA B Licence coach, currently undertaking his "A" Licence. Pert is also an FA Fitness Trainer and holder of a Masters Degree in Exercise Science. Pert is the coach of the U13 team at the Cambridge United Youth Academy.

Things to consider when planning a session:
- Progression
- Specificity
- Learning Styles
- Accelerated Learning - pre-learning, active learning and reflection
- Each drill lasts no more than 20 minutes in order to maintain player focus

First Session: Pre-Learning
The session begins with a story of a battle between the French and the English army. The English are outnumbered and are protecting a village, they are awaiting massive reinforcements. Therefore, they must not lose their position, but maintain it until those reinforcements arrive. What strategy should they employ?

Warm-Up
In a 20 x 20-yard area, with a number of cones placed randomly and with additional poles and mini hurdles, the warm-up begins with light jogging at different angles and dynamic movements. After 10 minutes of specific dynamic exercises, the players perform eight sprints. They work for 10 seconds and then rest for 20-30 seconds. The obstacles placed in the grid make sure different movements such as turning, acceleration and deceleration are performed under chaotic conditions with light jogging at different angles and dynamic movements. There are 12 players, so they work in pairs, in a passive sense, to begin with. One player with the ball moves forward across the width of the area shifting the ball from side to side. The partner gets low and works on changing the front foot as the ball changes from side to side. Each has three attempts as a defender. The progression is for the player with the ball to not only move from side to side, but also turn and move away from the defending partner, so that the defender learns to accelerate and close down an opponent when he turns to go toward his own goal.

1 v 1
In a 10 x 10-yard grid, pairs of players stand at each end and at each side. The practice begins with one player playing a pass across the grid to another player. That player can choose to play either a square or diagonal pass to one of the other two players. Once the pass has been made, the player who receives the ball tries to cross the line defended by the player who has not yet touched the ball. If the defending player wins the ball, he then looks to pass it to one of the other two players. Players then rotate roles.

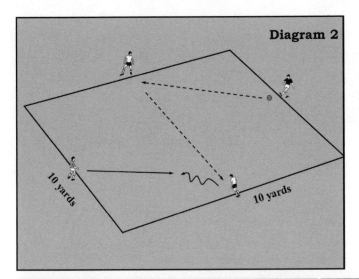

Diagram 2

Following the story at the start of practice, the players come up with eight points for 1 v 1 defending: *Anticipation; Acceleration; Line and Angle of Closing Down; Deceleration; Stance; Footwork; Intimidation and Tackling*

After 10 minutes, the players mark themselves on a scale of one to four (four being highest) on each defending point and then aim to improve on two particular points during the next 10 minutes. At the end of the 10 minutes the players give feedback to each other.

Cambridge United U13's

Defending Principles Drill

The next practice involves four players maintaining possession against two defenders, with the objective being to play the ball in between the two defenders in order to score a goal. The defenders objective is, therefore, to win back the ball, but also to prevent the ball from being played between them.

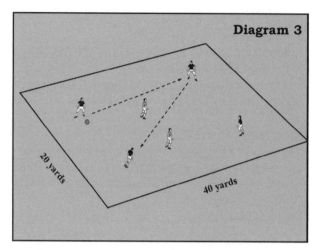

Diagram 3

Organization

In a 40 x 20-yard area, four attackers play against two defenders.

Coaching Points

- When to pressure the ball
- Support - angle and distance
- Intercepting - reading a player's intention, e.g. eye contact and movement of hips
- Communication - verbally and body language

Contextual Interference

Learning psychologists say that it is important to mix up practice so that when you go back to your main topic, the players have to go back into their memory and thus strengthen the connection in their brains. At this stage in the session, the players are given 15 minutes free time with the ball to work on an area of the game they want to improve.

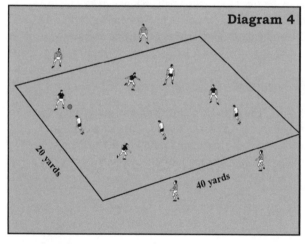

Diagram 4

Defending: Preventing the ball being played through

With three teams of four, two teams play while the other acts as target players. The target players then give feedback to the other two teams on their performance in the drill.

The black team plays against the whites in a 40 x 20-yard area. The objective is for the team in possession to play through the opposition by passing the ball to a target player outside the grid.

Progression

To begin with, the ball must be played along the ground to a target player. The progression is that the ball can then be played in the air to the target players. This helps the players learn where and when to pressure the ball or not.

Coaching Points

- Pressure the ball - when, where and how
- Support - distance and angles
- Compactness and Balance - width and depth
- Communication
- Recovery Runs - during transition from attack to defense

To warm down, the players work in pairs, 10 yards apart, and attempt to keep the ball up between themselves. When one player has the ball, the other jogs gently, performing light dynamic exercises around his partner.

Second Session: Pre-Learning

The pre-learning begins with asking the players in groups to think of a metaphor for penetration. Some of the answers include - water penetrating a rock or a nail into a wall. The next question asks the players to come up with similarities between the metaphors. The answers include holes (which we define as gaps) and filling the gaps. The groups discuss the objectives of counter-attacking to create gaps in the opposition's defense by moving them out of position and then filling gaps with the ball and players.

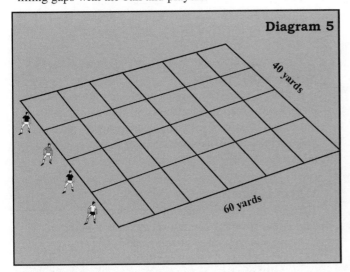

Diagram 5

40 yards

60 yards

Warm-Up

The outcome of the warm-up is to increase muscular temperature and to start the players focusing on special awareness while running forward. Players in a circle perform a number of dynamic drills, working from general warm-up drills to specific soccer specific exercises.

In a 60 x 40-yard area, with 24 grids marked off in 10 x 10-yard squares, players begin in lines of four at the top of the grid. On the coaches whistle, the first player sprints into any one of the 24 grids. The players can not run straight into the grid in front of them or to any grid where a teammates has moved into.

Progressions

- Add poles and mini hurdles to act as defenders, therefore increasing more specific soccer movements at pace, e.g. avoiding opponents, decelerating and re-accelerating.
- Add a ball. The ball can be dribbled into a grid or passed into a grid ahead of a player's run.

Team Building Exercise

A grid is set up with nine 2 x 2-yard squares. Eight players will occupy a square leaving one square free. The coach gives each player a number and then tells them the numbers of each grid square. The players have to find a solution for each player to be in the corresponding grid number by moving around. One square can only contain one player at a time. Although the drill is not specific to soccer, it teaches players to solve problems for themselves and also think moves ahead.

Contextual Interference

1 v 1 attacking plus a goalkeeper. For 10 minutes the players perform 1 v 1 against a partner in 10 x 10 -yard grids outside of the penalty area. If they go past their partner they get the chance to shoot at goal.

Counter-Attacking Drill

The area of play is from one goal line to the other side of the center circle. In an area of 40 x 20-yards, players play 6 v 5. The team of five (white team) try to keep possession in order to dribble the ball over the end line. The team of six (black team), once they win possession, attempt to counter attack with two options. They can play the ball into an area marked out for one of the strikers to show into, or they can play a pass to one of the players wide of the main playing area. Once the ball is played out of the grid, two more players from the black team can join in the attack, together with one of the white defenders.

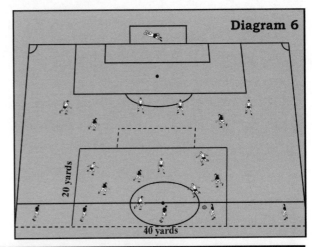

Diagram 6

20 yards

40 yards

Coaching Points - Attacking Team
- Win the ball
- Secure possession - ideally forward, pass appreciation i.e. Can the player play without having a touch?
- Receiving skills - body shape, awareness, letting the ball run
- Movement - support in front of the ball (attacking space, pulling defenders out to create gaps, attacking the gaps)
- Running with the ball and pass quality - in front of the supporting player, disguise and timing of the release
- End product and rebounds

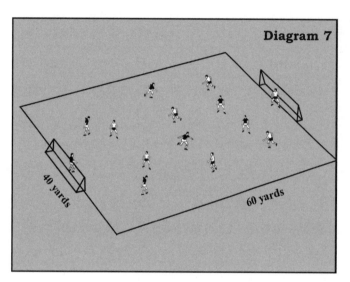

Diagram 7

40 yards

60 yards

Small-Sided Game
In a 60 x 40-yard grid, two teams of six plus goalkeepers play a small-sided game with small "five-a-side" goals. The coach reemphasizes a couple of coaching points of the session every five minutes during any quick drink breaks.

Warm Down
The players are in groups of five with one ball in a small circle. The players attempt to keep the ball in the air and have a maximum of three touches. They must pass the ball to a teammate not directly next to them, jog around the player they have just passed to and the player who next receives the ball, before returning to their original position. The drill is performed for six to eight minutes and maintains player concentration while also reducing their body temperature.

Derek Broadley

Contributed by Derek Broadley, former Academy Director at Crystal Palace F.C. of the English First Division and now National Director of Coaching for Premier Skills, a coach education company. Broadley is also the President of www. soccer-expert.com. This session is geared toward young players from the ages of 8 to 12, but with an increased or decreased area size, can be used across different age ranges. This session can be seen in a video format at www.soccer-expert.com.

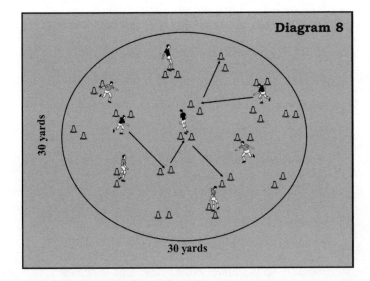

Diagram 8

30 yards

30 yards

Activity One: Staying with the ball

The area used does not need to be a specific shape, however, the area size has to be big enough for the players to understand the set up and to allow for the skills to be performed with sufficient "Time and Space". The area should be 30 x 30-yards with at least 45 gates of different colors (Gates = 2 cones). Each player will get into a gate of their choice as their starting point. The players are then instructed to jog slowly in a sequence of colors through the gates.

Coaching Points
- Run with head up
- Plan your route
- Maintain a constant speed

Progression

Ask the players to perform different movements in their sequence, guided by different colored gates (e.g. green to blue; hopping, blue to red; skipping, red to green; running backwards etc). Coaches should look at the quality of the movement and refer to speed (Most players will go too fast!). The coach can select certain movements after the players have had an opportunity to experiment.

Progression

Ask the players to perform different speeds in their sequence, guided by the different colored gates (e.g. green to red; fast, blue to green; jogging etc). Coaches can give examples and demonstrate. Players must avoid each other and they cannot go through a gate that is occupied by someone else. Although players have a sequence, they must make decisions based on the actions of the players around them.

Activity Two: Staying with the ball

Using the same area and set up, players now have a ball in their starting gate. Players are asked to run with the ball in a sequence through the colored gates as in the previous activity.

Coaching Points

Run with the head up, keeping control of the ball and planning a route.

Progression

Ask the players to use alternate feet in the sequence (i.e green to blue, right foot; blue to red; left foot, etc). Coaches watch individuals to see if they can maintain their sequence. Coaches should encourage good speed. "Who is the quickest?" This will aid movement, but must not compromise quality.

Progression

Ask the players to use the outside of the foot once they exit the gate to change direction to the next gate. Coaches will be able to see when a player is making the decision on the direction of the next gate. (Coaches should coach individuals without stopping the players who are coping with the task.)

Progression
Ask the players to choose a color in their sequence and when they approach that color, don't go through that gate. (They have to do a turn and avoid going through).

Activity Three: Staying with the ball
Put players in pairs and number them 1 and 2. Player one does not have a ball. Player one jogs slowly through a sequence and is followed by player two, who runs with their ball. (If odd numbers, get a group of three with players two and three following player one).

Coaching Points
• Run with the head up
• Keep close to the player you are following
• Keep control of the ball
• Avoid contact with other players

Coaches to encourage the player without the ball to maintain a constant speed and not to turn around and look for other players. Also, encourage long and short runs between gates.

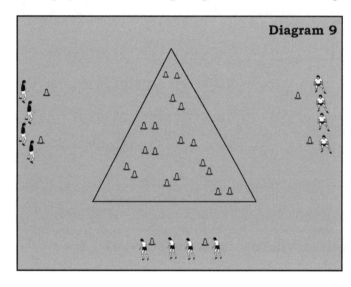

Diagram 9

Activity Four: Staying with the ball
Split the group into three teams. Three small goals are placed around a triangular area with the three groups placed in set positions. Place gates in the triangular area 15-18-yards away from each of the three goals. Give each player a number between 1 and 4. When the coach calls out a number, the player who's number is called, has to run with the ball through a sequence of gates before heading for a goal to score.

Coaching Points
• Run with the head up
• Plan your route
• Keep the ball under control
• Score at earliest opportunity
• Can add more goals to keep waiting time down

Activity Five: Staying with the ball
Using a field 60 x 40-yards with goals at either end, the group is split equally in number. Place gates around the wide areas of the field.

The objective is to play a regular game, with additional goals being awarded if a player can successfully run through a gate maintaining possession of the ball.

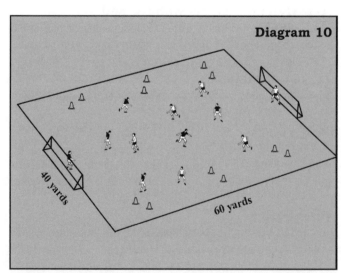

Diagram 10

40 yards

60 yards

Wimbledon F.C.

These sessions were observed by Daryn "Ozzie" White, Director of Coaching for Ankeny S.C. in Iowa, along with Sean Kehoe. Wimbledon F.C. is currently in the English First Division and have become the first club in British soccer to re-locate their franchise from South London to Milton Keynes. Under the guidance of manager Stuart Myrdoch, 1st team coach Jimmy Gilligan, Academy Director Martin Heather and Under 19's coach, Gary Smith, the following sessions were samples of the daily routine of some of the teams within the club.

Under 15's

In a 15 x 15-yard grid, six to eight players play keep-away from two defenders placed in the middle of the area. Touches were limited to one, two or mandatory three.

Coaching Points
- Body shape
- Quick feet
- Decision making

After 15 minutes of work, the group breaks for some stretching.

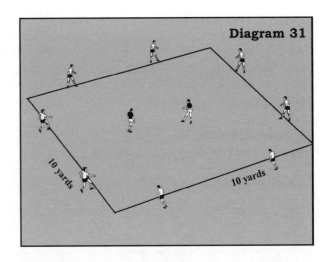

Diagram 31

10 yards
10 yards

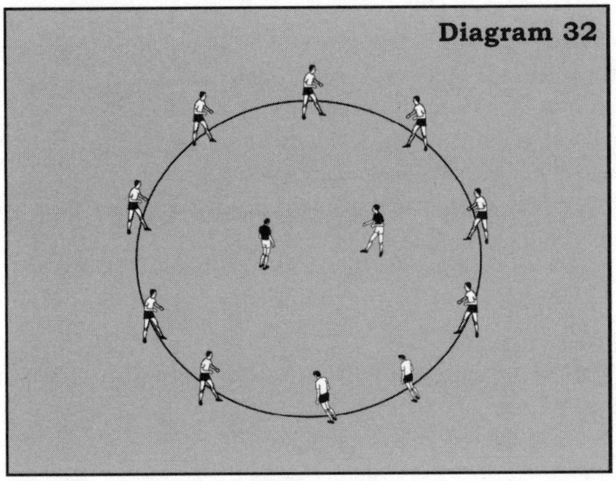

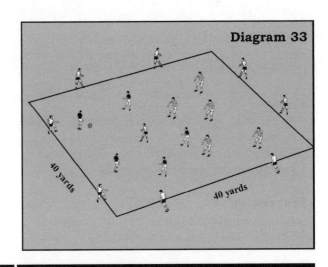

Diagram 32

Progression

Players on the outside now hold hands forming a circle and move in a circular motion, again trying to keep the ball away from the one or two defenders placed in the middle.

Progression

Using the same circle and no defenders, the players juggled the ball using any body part initially, then moving onto to headers only, and finally some sequence juggling e.g. foot - thigh - head.

Following the juggling, the players move onto to complete some speed and agility work using ladders.

5 v 5 + Targets

In a 40 x 40-yard area, players play 5 v 5 + 1 with two target players placed on each side of the area. Target players only have one touch while the remaining players use two.

Coaching Points
- Pace of pass
- Stretch area, make the space as big as possible
- Play the ball forward quickly: penetrate
- Body shape
- As the ball travels, support players should fix angles and distances
- Think two or three moves ahead

Diagram 33

40 yards
40 yards

Wimbledon F.C.

5 v 5 + 1 with Target's

Using a 40 x 30-yard area, players play 5 v 5 + 1 to two small goals. Target players are now placed in each corner of the field and are allowed to move between cones, changing angles for receiving and returning passes.

Rules and Restrictions

The neutral player is restricted to one, two or unlimited touches. The target players are restricted to one touch. The 10 other players play two-touch. If a goal is scored in open play, one point is awarded, if a team scores after using a target player, three points are awarded.

Coaching Points

- Play forward quickly
- Penetrate early
- Support the ball as it travels
- Decision making

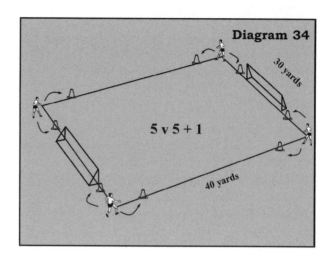

Diagram 34

5 v 5 + 1

30 yards

40 yards

Wimbledon Reserve Team

Players are split into two groups. One group undertakes some circuit training using a ball, the other play small-sided games.

Group One

The circuit works both clockwise and counter-clockwise. Using a series of checking movements, give-and-go's, pass-and-follow, the white team plays passes within the circuit. Players receiving the ball are encouraged to show for a pass to feet, check from in front and behind a passive defender and take touches in the direction of the next pass.

Coaching Points

- Visual cues - triggers
- Timing of the run and pass
- Weight of the pass
- Deception and the receiving technique

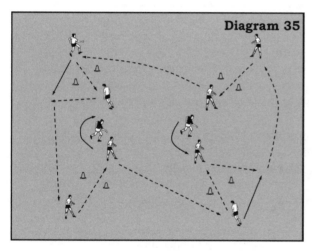

Diagram 35

Group Two

Play a 4 v 4 small-sided game with target players placed at each end of the area.

Rules

- Five connecting passes equals one point (one to two-touch restriction)
- Play a pass to a target player in-between the coned goals, following a give-and-go combination

Progression

- Keep possession and change direction after scoring
- Find the target player with an aerial pass

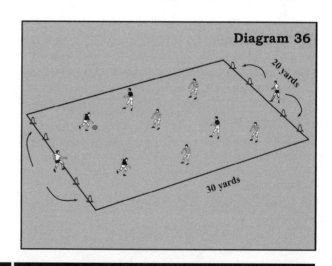

Diagram 36

20 yards

30 yards

Wimbledon F.C.

First Team: Warm-Up

The players do 15 minutes of various soccer movements: ballistics, stretching, mind games such as Simon Says, Opposites, etc. The team is then split into two, with one group undertaking some functional training and the other playing a series of small-sided games. For the functional session, using a 4:5:1 formation, the coach uses two full backs, two central midfielders, two wide midfielders, one center forward and one goalkeeper.

Objective

- Penetrate early and create space for the central midfielders to join the attack
- Find the center forward to begin the attacks from the flanks and to create crossing opportunities

Ball Movement

The coach serves to one of two central midfielders. The CM plays it to a fullback and the fullback plays it up to the center forward. The CF lays it off to a wide midfielder and checks into the penalty area. The wide midfielder makes room for a cross. The two CM's decide who joins the CF in the penalty area and who stays on the edge of the box.

(The CF can hold the ball up and lay it off to a CM who plays the ball wide).

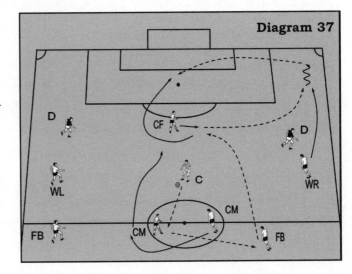

Coaching Points

- Visual cues
- Timing of pass
- Timing of runs
- Quality of the long pass (must bypass the oppositions midfield, but drop in front of the center forward)
- Everything to be played at game pace

(This session was practiced on a Thursday prior to the Saturday game in which they beat Bradford City, using this system).

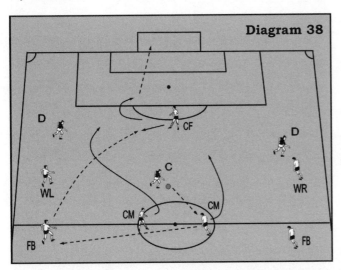

Option Two

Coach serves to the CM, CM to FB, FB to CF with the WMF making a run inside as the ball travels. CF holds, spins and shoots, or, alternatively holds and lays the ball off for the oncoming WMF.

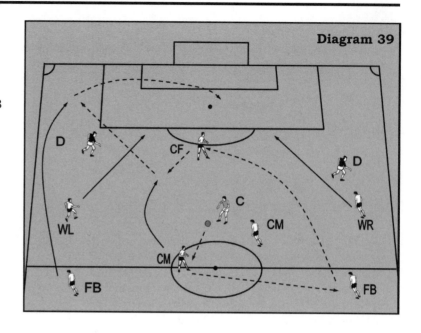

Diagram 39

Option Three

Coach serves to the CM, CM to the FB. The FB finds the CF with a long pass. The opposite FB moves forward on an overlapping run. The CF lays the ball off to the supporting CM who switches play by playing the overlapping FB into space for the cross.

Every session we observed ended with some speed ladders, hurdles, speed production activities and agilities.

Counter-Attacking

This session, which focuses on counter-attacking, was submitted by Bill Swartz, Head Coach of the Pomona-Pitzer College. The session is a combination of English F.A., Queens Park Rangers and Watford F.C. practices observed by Swartz during a stint he had at the Watford F.C. Academy.

Counter-Attacking is the result of an interception, challenges won, recovery challenges and loose or 50/50 balls won. Training sessions should emphasize looking immediately for any chance to counter, a sense of urgency on and off the ball, to get forward, and attacking as quickly as possible under control. If there is no opportunity for the counter-attack, the team should try and maintain possession and build an attack from there.

Developing Interpassing and Quick Attacking Play

Play 6 v 3 plus a 2 v 1 in a 40 x 20-yard area. The coach plays the ball to any defender in a 20 x 10-yard area. The defenders only have one touch to encourage turnovers. The attackers look to win the ball and then 'run' the ball out to attack the defender and either goal at speed. The attackers only have six seconds to score once in the 2 v 1 situation.

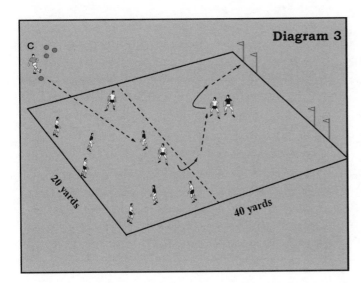

Diagram 3

20 yards

40 yards

Coaching Points
- Look for positive attacking attitudes
- Encourage creativity and demand communication
- Create space by committing a defender.
- If an attacker attacks centrally, there is space on either side to attack
- If the ball carrier attacks down the line, space is available on the opposite side

Progression
- Introduce off sides
- Add recovering defender(s)
- Add a full sized goal
- Build to a 3 v 2 situation

Developing Interpassing and Quick Attacking Play
5 v 5 plus 1 v 1 Full Field

The coach starts the practice by playing the ball to the defenders (white). The white team looks to maintain possession. When the black team wins the ball, they have two passes to play the ball forward to X1. If getting the ball to X1 is not "ON", the X's maintain possession and the white team looks to win the ball back and play to O1 in one or two passes. One player from the attacking team can join X1 or O1 in an attack on goal.

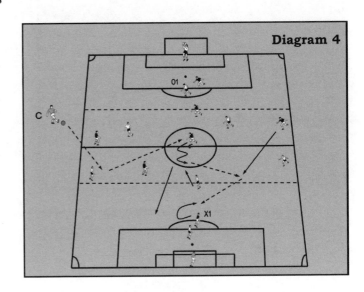

Diagram 4

Coaching Points
- Positive attacking attitude by all
- Quality runs by X1 and O1 to get free of markers
- Quality pass into X1/O1 and the speed and quality of the supporting player(s)
- The urgency to strike at the goal

Counter-Attacking

Progression

- One player from the attacking team can join X1/O1
- Off side in effect
- If the goalkeeper makes a save, he can initiate an attack by throwing to a midfielder
- If "ON" the X's or O's can RUN the ball into the attack
- Add recovering defender(s)
- Build to 3 v 2, 4 v 3, etc.

Reshaping During a Counter Attack 8 v 6 - Working With a 4-4-2 Shape

Teams are most vulnerable to counters while they are countering. It is vital to cover this aspect with your team when using this type of practice. Defenders look to win all long balls. Midfielders look to win all short balls. When the ball is won, it is immediately played to the coach. At least two players attack beyond the coach (attacking the back of the defense). The team must tactically reshape during the counter while the fullbacks serve and support players. Later they will be allowed to recover.

Coaching Points

- Central defenders must communicate and help reshape the team
- Midfielders must look over their shoulders to see where opposition forwards are checking to. This will assist with interceptions
- If the two central midfielders "Go", the outside midfielders must tuck in. In all situations, the center must be strong against possible re-counter

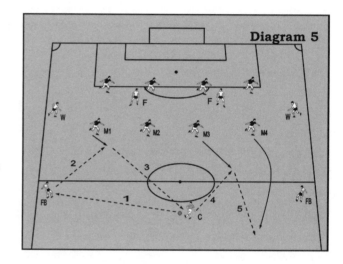

Diagram 5

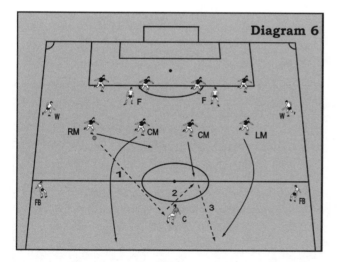

Diagram 6

Progression(s)

- Add a goal and goalkeeper
- Add a defender, who may counter if the ball is won
- Add a linesman
- Allow the wide FB's to recover

After playing an attacking pass to the coach, the right midfielder steps inside to cover for the right central midfielder who has made a deep attacking run, re-establishing the shape centrally.

Counter-Attacking

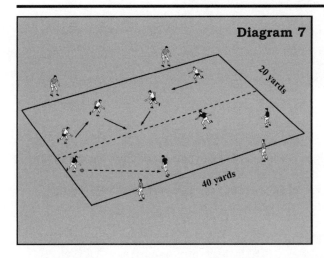

Diagram 7

Practicing Defensive Positioning

The X's (white's) as a team, look to show the O's (black's) inside as shown. All X's must show defensive patience, while the O's will be allowed possession in their own half of the field.

Practice teaching midfielders to look over their shoulders to see the opposition's positioning (use a 40 x 20-yard grid to practice this). X's maintain possession playing one or two-touch, looking to give a penetration pass to their targets. O's look to intercept or block any through passes. O's must check over their shoulders to see where the X targets are. The targets may move along the line.

Defending Deep To Counter-Attack

System of play used: 4-4-2 versus a 3-5-2. The coach begins the practice by passing the ball to the O's goalkeeper. The coach dictates where and how the goalkeeper distributes the ball (throw/kick). This will allow the X's to establish their defensive priorities. In this example, the X's are in an attacking 4-4-2 shape, drop off and establish a 4-2-3-1 defensive shape.

The X's, as a team, must show the O's inside and all X's must show defensive patience. O's will be allowed possession and the X goalkeeper will adopt the correct starting position in relationship to where the O goalkeeper plays the ball.

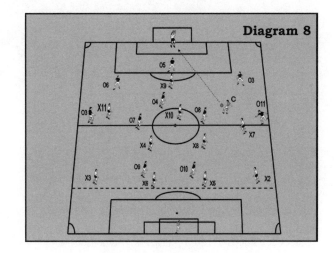

Diagram 8

Points of Emphasis

- X9 must only press if there is a good chance to win the ball. If not, X9 will get in a good position to receive a pass if the ball is won by the players behind him
- X11 and X7 will "tuck in" and "drop in" behind X9 in order to show the O's inside
- X10's job is very important to potential counters. X10 screens in front of X4 and X8 in the central area. X10 will make diagonal runs on counters
- X4 and X8 work together in front of the two central defenders X5 and X6. (They must be trained to "look" over their shoulders to know where O9 and O10 are). Their major job is to stop the O central midfielders from turning
- X10, X11, X7, X4 and X8 look to win (intercept) the short balls. At the very least, they will work to not allow their markers to turn
- The back four (X2,3,5 and 6) will hold a deep line (coned off). They will look, in order of defensive priority to intercept, spoil (the attackers first touch) or jockey. When the ball is won, they will look for forward passes to X9, X10, X11, X7 or X4 and X8. Failing this they will maintain possession
- The goalkeepers will constantly adjust starting position and will offer communication to the back four. The two central defenders are responsible for communication to X4 and X8 and communication continues up the field
- When the ball is won, the X's should counter immediately. If they cannot, they must try to maintain possession

Progression(s)

- Play begins with the coach playing to one of the O back players, then midfielders and then the forwards
- Play starts with X's. When X's lose the ball, defend to counter
- Free play

Defending With a Back Four

Wayne Harrison, Director of Player and Coach Development at the Eden Prairie Soccer Club in Minnesota, submitted the following sessions based on developing play with a defending back four. The session is designed to show how to work on team shape, building up from a back four.

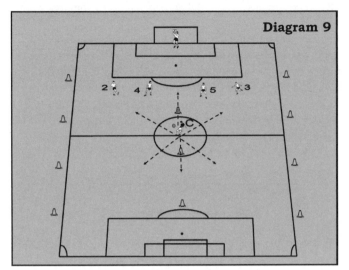

Traveling With The Ball

Side cones are 20 to 25 yards apart, as are the defenders and the coach. The coach moves with the ball and the defenders mirror the movement, maintaining the distances between them.

The coach can use signal words such as UP, OUT, HOLD, DROP, SLIDE to determine the movement. Eventually, you need to work up to an 11 v 11 situation, showing how to work a team as individuals, as units and ultimately as a team.

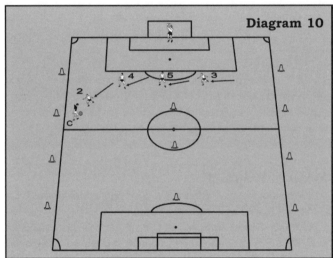

In this example, the coach moves to the outside and the whole back four adjust (slide) their positions across the field to compensate for this movement, with player 2 being the one to apply immediate pressure on the ball.

The coach needs to re-emphasize the idea that the players are tied as links on a chain and so move together as links of a unit. (The coach, in some instances, can tie the players together so they know how it feels when they move together).

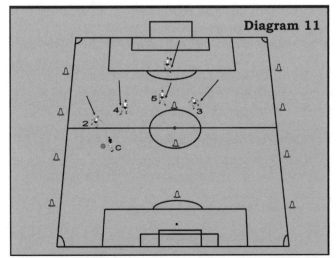

The coach moves back up the field and the back four unit moves up based on the position of the ball. Player 2 is still the pressing player so he must stay close to the ball should the coach turn.

Defending With a Back Four

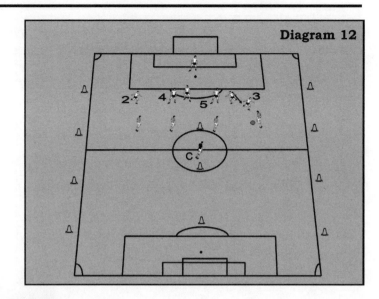

Diagram 12

The attacking players pass the ball across their line and in front of the defenders. The defenders adjust their positions to mirror this movement. This is working on marking zones and marking players and distinguishing between the two, depending on where the ball is.

Following every pass, the play is halted to check the defender's positions.

The side cones are used as guides in terms of distancing between units as they are introduced.

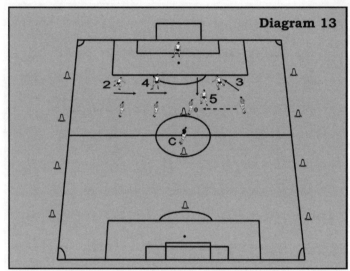

Diagram 13

As the ball is passed inside, the defenders adjust, closing down the player on the ball and closing down the spaces around the ball. This is continued using all the players, sometimes missing a player with a pass, so it goes across two players to test the defenders.

Once they have grasped this concept, the next progression can be introduced.

Introducing Opponents For The Defenders To Shadow

The coach now has players to pass to. These players initially must be static to check the set up. Players maintain an open stance so they can see opponents as well as the ball. When the ball is at C or D, the back four take up positions with regard to A and B, and do not get drawn to the ball. The defending team can win back the ball only with interceptions of passes (and not with tackles) so that the shape can be monitored.

Introduce targets (T's) for the defenders to pass to should they win the ball.

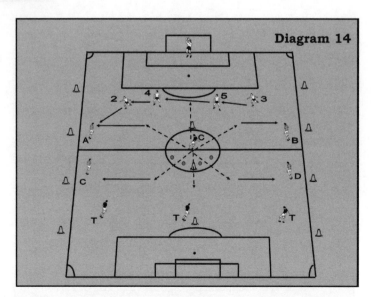

Diagram 14

Defending With a Back Four

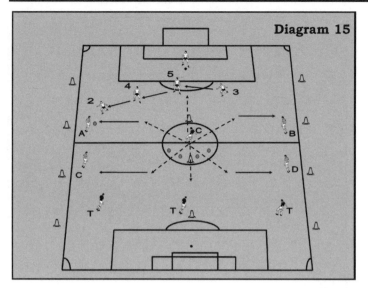

Diagram 15

Once the ball has been passed wide, the back four slide into position. Notice that the back four is NOT flat, but rather angled and linked between each player, with the central defender the deepest player. This player can effectively be called the "Sweeper". When the ball is at B on the other side, player 4 becomes the sweeper. The second center back is the deepest player and the two center backs share this responsibility, depending on which side of the field the ball is positioned.

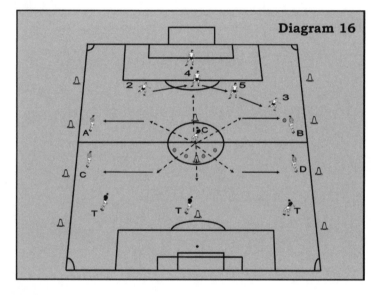

Diagram 16

In this example, the ball has been transferred to the other side of the field and the back four have adjusted accordingly. The sweeper is now Player 4, and the further from the ball, the more they mark space.

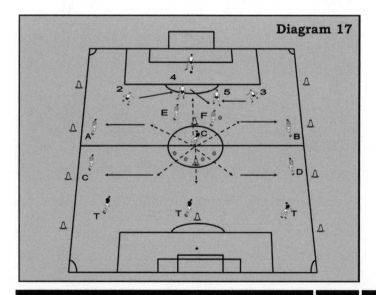

Diagram 17

Introduce two strikers on the attacking team to check the positions of the defenders with more choices of where the ball is on the field. The strikers now offer more options of passes, and the defending players more decisions to make. (The coach should stop/freeze the play at any time to check defenders positioning).

Defenders continue to position themselves based on the position of the ball, their immediate opponent and the goal. At the same time they must maintain their shape to ensure there are no holes created between them for the opposition to exploit.

Defending With a Back Four

Introduce a Midfield Four On The Defending Team

Introduce the same shape midfield as the back four. Try to maintain the same distance (about 5 to 10 yards) between the back four and the midfield four as they move up and down the field. Maintain the same distances between the players and the position of the ball up to the half way line.

The midfield players use the same principles of adjustment as the back four, maintaining their shape and keeping tight around the position of the ball.

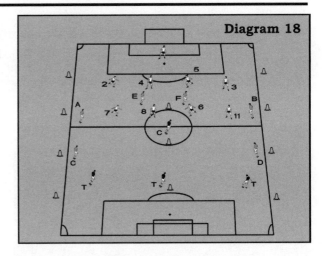

The midfield adjusts as the ball is passed to player D. Number 11 closes, 8 drops in to support, 6 and 7 squeeze across. The back four push up and across to maintain the distance between themselves and the midfield. Number 8 could double up on D with player 11 as an option.

Player D passes the ball to the coach again, the ball is switched to another player and the defenders adjust again as a team to compensate. The wide players remain static, just receiving and passing. Defenders can still only intercept passes. If they win the ball with an interception they can try to hit a target player (T) to score.

The positions of the players, after they have adjusted to the pass to D, shows number 11 being the pressing player, showing D inside to the defensive support. By the time the ball is transferred across the field to player C, the defending team can travel, as the ball travels, with time to get across. The immediate danger areas are the spaces around the ball, and they need to be filled as shown.

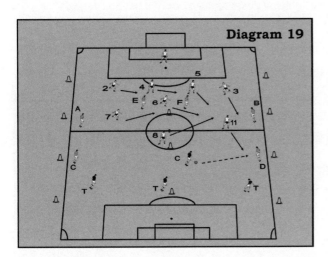

Tactical Design Plan

- Pressure
- Support
- Cover/Balance
- Recover
- Double Team
- Track
- Compactness

Introduce two midfielders and allow all the players to play with no restrictions. The coach picks up on any faults as they happen in open play, correcting and re-positioning the players. When the defending team wins an interception, they can pass to the targets.

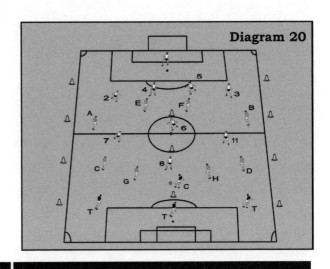

Defending With a Back Four

Five Things a Midfielder Has To Think About

- *Recover* back and get *goal side*
- Be the *pressurizing player* to stop the player on the ball (win, delay or force one way)
- *Support* the pressurizing player with angle, distance and communication
- Cover their *own opponent,* so as they receive the ball, they can close them down
- *Step into passing lanes* to prevent forward passes

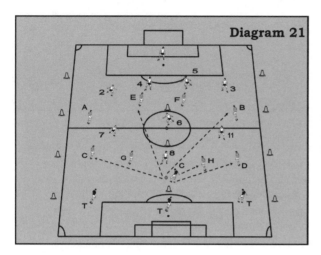

Once the players get used to the tactical plan, allow the defenders to tackle opponents and win the ball back, as in a game. The coach can pass the ball to various attacking players in different positions on the field and the defending team must try to regain possession and get the ball to a target.

4 v 8 With Recovering Midfielders

Make the defensive challenge more difficult by starting the midfield in recovering positions. The back four can be patient when the ball is in the midfield, and keep their shape, delaying the opponents until the midfield recover back. (Have a time limit before they can begin that recovery).

Progression

Start by using four recovering midfielders, then make it increasingly difficult by using only two, then just have the back four defending against eight attackers.

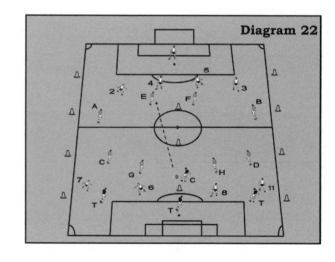

4 v 8 Overload Situations

In setting up this situation, you are really testing whether or not the back four have grasped the defensive concepts you have coached. Players now need to decide when to mark a player and when to mark space.

Pay particular attention to the wide defenders being drawn to close down players C or D and leave A and B free, thus breaking up the shape and offering opportunities to the attacking team to get behind the defense in wide areas. Also, observe the central players being drawn into midfield. Patience is the key here.

Defending With a Back Four

Too Close Or Not Too Close In Wide Areas

The best course of action is for the back four to stay intact and allow the midfielders of the attacking team to play and pass the ball in front of them. They should only attempt to close players down as they get closer to the goal or the ball gets closer to their immediate opponents. In this example, C gets the ball but is in no danger, therefore, player number 2 holds his position aware of where C is, but moves across the field slightly closer to A, just in case A receives the ball. If the ball is passed to A, then 2 has to close A down. The rest of the back four moves slightly across also, maintaining distances.

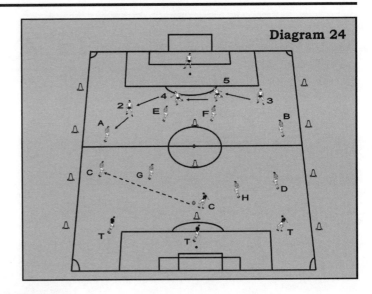

Diagram 24

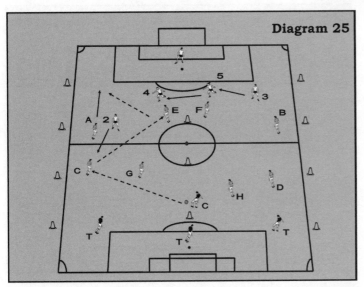

Diagram 25

This example shows what can happen if the wide defender is drawn to the ball when it is with player C. Player 2 leaves the space and closes down on C, the ball is passed into striker E, who can lay the ball wide into open space for A to run into unopposed. This now compromises 4's position, who now has a 2 v 1 situation. If 2 were to anticipate the pass early and be in position to intercept, only then would it be possible to close C down and have success. (If the four defenders were tied together, it would prevent this situation from happening.)

Too Close Or Not Too Close In Central Areas

The best course of action when the position of a central player is threatened by the striker coming short for the ball, is for player number 5 to only go so far before letting the striker (F) go deep into midfield. In a game situation, a midfielder should pick up F on entering their zone.

As 5 goes short, 4 becomes extra cover and moves across to cover the space left by 5; 2 moves across to cover the space left by 4, leaving the outside space free. The best scenario is for 5 to only go so far, then drop back to establish the chain link of the back four again.

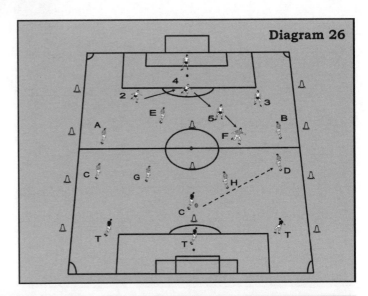

Diagram 26

Defending With a Back Four

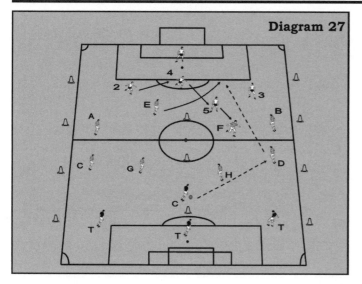

Diagram 27

A position to avoid getting into would be when the striker goes short to receive the ball to feet, and the defender (5) goes too far into the midfield, leaving space in behind for the second striker to move diagonally into. Should this happen, players 2 and 4 need to move across to cover and fill the spaces.

Defending In An 11 v 11 Situation

The coach serves to the opponents in different locations and the defending team tries to win the ball back individually and collectively. The objective of the defending team when they win the ball could be just to chip the ball into the opponents goalkeeper.

Zonal defending as a team, using a 4-3-1-2 system of play, with a diamond shape midfield, is shown in this example, but the same principles apply with other systems using zonal methods of defending. The session can be set up in any team's preferred system of play, or a team can set up the other team in the system of play that your next opponents use to practice defending against.

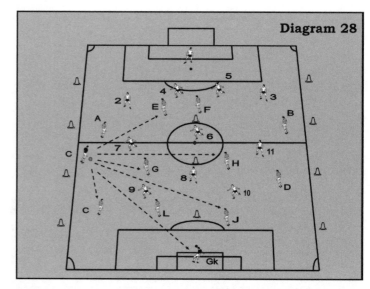

In this example, a 4-4-2 system is set up to defend against, with the coach playing the ball into various situations to initiate attacks.

This allows many opportunities for defensive situations to practice, the defending team can now be allowed to attack the opposition as a reward for regaining possession and score a goal if possible.

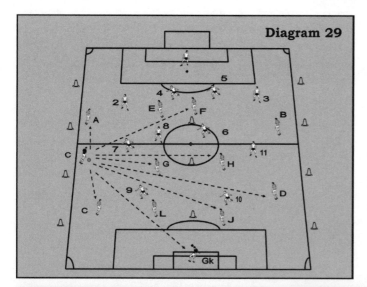

Golden Goal

This goal was scored by Brian McClair for Manchester United in a game against Chelsea during the 1991 - 1992 season. It highlights how effective restarts, in this case a throw-in, can be for creating goal chances. Only the players involved are shown so as not to clutter the diagram.

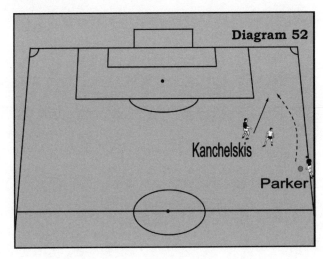

Paul Parker takes the throw-in and throws it down the line for a running Kanchelskis. Kanchelskis holds the ball up and then plays it back for Parker.

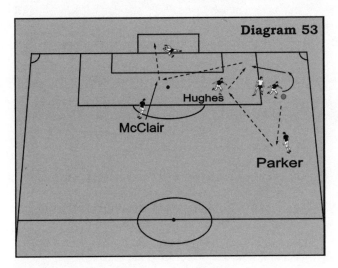

Parker plays a firm pass into the feet of Mark Hughes. Hughes holds the ball up, protecting it from a defender who is marking him tightly.

In the meantime, Kanchelskis has made a curved, overlapping run. Hughes sees this, and back-heels the ball into his path. Kanchelskis crosses the ball with one touch for an incoming Brian McClair to side foot into the goal with one touch.

Everton F.C.

This session is contributed by James Clarkson. Clarkson observed Everton during their pre-season training sessions in Houston, Texas. Each session was conducted with a high level of intensity and all the players wore heart monitors. Fourteen outfield players trained with Head Coach David Moyes and his assistant Alan Irvine.

Warm-Up

The players complete three gentle laps around the field and stretch. They then perform eight, 60-yard runs at full speed.

Players perform:
- 20 yard sprint
- Inside cut and 20 yard sprint
- Inside cut and 20-yard diagonal sprint
- Two players race at the same time
- Next two players in line go after first cut

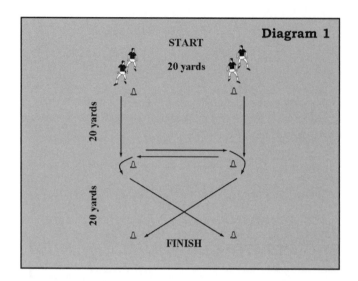

Keep-Away

Players play 7 v 2 in one grid with five players resting in the other grid.

Each new game starts with the coach playing the first pass. Alternate the two chasers after each go. Play two-touch, then following every 10 passes, add another chaser and reduce to a one-touch limit.

There must be one player from the passing team playing in the "hole" (middle of the box).

The chasers try and knock the ball out of the box.

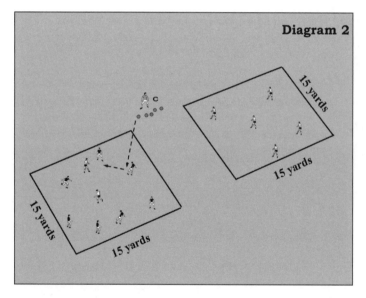

Progressions
- Players must follow their pass
- Players must exit and enter the box after every pass
- Finish with normal play

Coaching Points
- Communication
- Positive touches and passes
- Quality of the recovery runs of the two chasers

Directional Possession (Four-Goal Game)

The game is played in one half of the field with small goals or cones placed as shown, six yards in from the line.

Play 5 v 5 (+2). Each team has a target player in opposite diagonal goals.

Teams must keep possession from one target to the other. Players **MUST** have two touches. Change target players every two minutes.

Progressions

- Unlimited touches inside - target players are one-touch.
- 6 v 6 (+2). Same game as before, except the two neutral players are on the field and play for the team in possession.

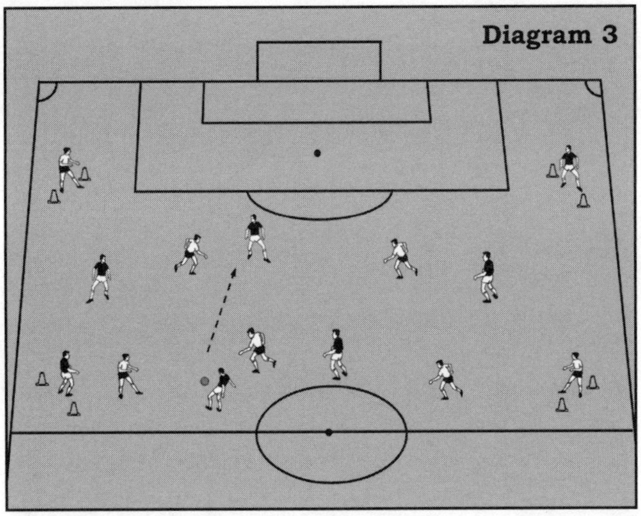

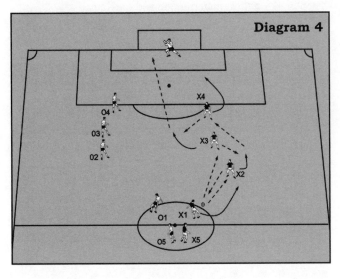

Diagram 3

Diagram 4

Shooting

With the same teams from the previous exercise, the players are placed into positions as shown.

- X1 passes diagonally to X2
- X2 passes back to X1 and spins out
- X1 passes to X3
- X3 passes to X2 and spins out
- X2 passes to X4
- X4 lays off for X3 to shoot
- X4 follows in for rebound

- Each player moves up a spot and X5 will start
- Alternate each side (same routine on both sides)
- Players look to finish in the opposite corner of the goal

Coaching Points

- Sharp speed and quality passes
- Don't run across the ball when you return pass it

Conditioning

Fig. 1
The whole team works together, sprinting flat out for 30 yards, with a 14 second rest between sprints.

Fig. 2
Players get into pairs and perform:
- 10 yard sprint
- 10 yard jog
- 20 yard sprint

Eight runs of each circuit are completed.

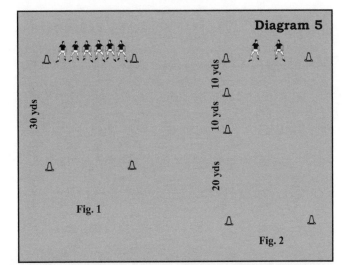

Diagram 5

Everton F.C.

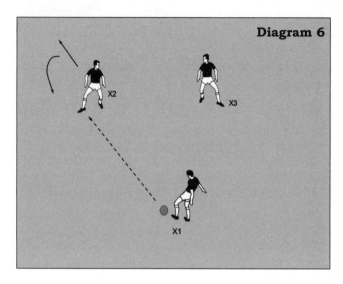

Diagram 6

Passing & Moving

In three's, approximately 10 yards apart, the players perform the following exercises:
- Control and pass
- Check away a yard, control and pass
- Check in, half turn, control and pass

Progressions:

Players have three choices, **"Hold It"**, **"Man On"**, and **"Turn."** The passer calls out instructions to the receiving player.
- **"Hold it"** - control and pass to other player
- **"Man on"** - control and return ball to passer
- **"Turn"** - must use different turns before passing to other player

Add in **"Through You"** - under hit pass, let it run and turn. Then work on third man running and overlaps.

Team Shape

Working on team shape (back four and two holding center midfielders) with 7 v 9 playing full field.

Defending team (black) lines up with a goalkeeper, back four and two holding midfielders. Attacking team (white) lines up with three defenders, four midfielders, and two forwards.

Ball starts with the white defenders as they try to score playing regular soccer. If the defending team wins the ball, they try and score using the movements from the previous exercises.

When the defending team has the ball, the center midfielders must keep shape and space (don't come in and show too early).

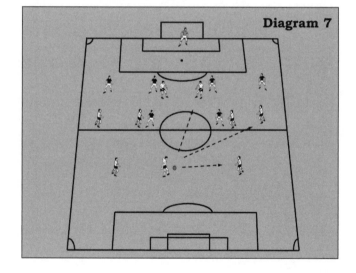

Diagram 7

Coaching Points
- Focus on defensive shape
- Center midfielders work from side to side and don't chase the ball
- Fullbacks push out and pressure wide midfielders
- Center backs mark on the outside shoulder of forwards (goal side, ball side)
- Cut off channels and through balls
- Counter attack at speed with quality movement off the ball

Everton F.C.

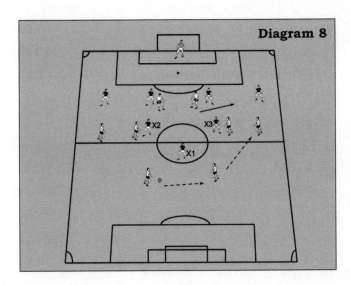

Diagram 8

Team Shape

Continuing with team shape, change the formations to 8 v 8 by moving the attacking teams center back to play on the defensive team as an attacking midfielder. Play the same game as before.

Coaching Points

- If the white team defenders have the ball, X1 (attacking mid) pressures the ball and X2 and X3 (defensive mid) must fill in the holes behind X1 to cut out any through balls
- If X2 or X3 pushes out and pressures, X1 must drop into defensive position

Every time the ball goes out of bounds, the coach shows every player their starting positions and walks through what their responsibilities are.

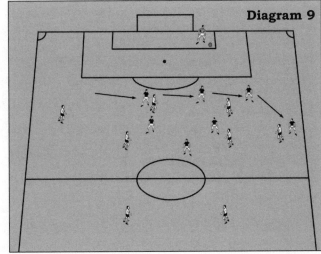

Diagram 9

Team Shape

New starting positions from a defensive goal kick on the left side.

Push the left back into wide mid position. The center back moves across to left back and the right back moves into the middle with other center back.

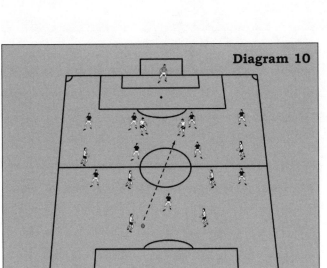

Diagram 10

Team Shape

Continuing with team shape, change the team formations to 10 v 8 with the defensive team now having the numerical advantage.

Add two wide players that play higher than the defensive midfielders.

Everton F.C.

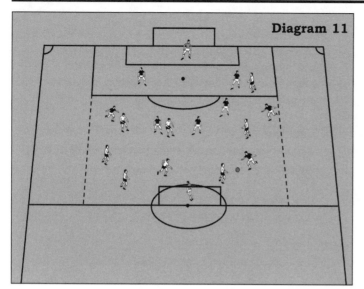

Diagram 11

Practice Game

The players are divided into teams to play a 9 v 9 on half a field. The width of the field is the same as the width of the 18-yard area.

The game is played with a two-touch condition and is very competitive, with no interruption from the coaches.

Crossing and Finishing

- Play starts with X1 playing the ball to X2
- X2 returns the ball to X1, who then plays the ball diagonally to X4
- X4 controls and crosses the ball for X1 and X2
- Play is then reversed with X2 playing to X1 and the ball going out the opposite side to X3

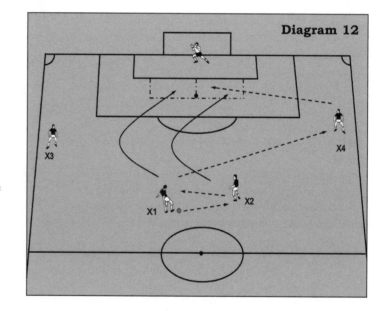

Diagram 12

Coaching Points

- Goalkeeper cannot enter second six-yard area
- Forwards must time runs into the second six-yard area
- Second six-yard area is split into two boxes, near and far
- Players must have two touches - quality preparation touch, and then strike, pass or cross
- Variation with crosses, lofted, bent, near and far, but must hit second six-yard box
- The timing of runs starts with the crossers first touch

Sam Saif

This session was conducted by Sam Saif at the February, 2004 WORLD CLASS COACHING International Coaching Seminar in Kansas City. These exercises are from sessions conducted by Saif at the Sheffield United F.C. Academy with his U15 team.

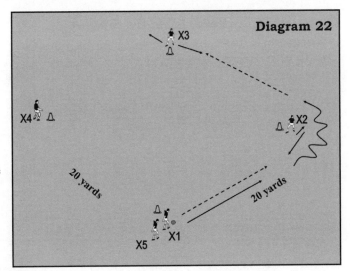

Diamond Drill - Passing & Turning

In the following diagrams, five players are lined up in a diamond formation 20 yards apart. Each drill begins with X1 starting with the ball.

- X1 begins by passing to X2 and follows the pass
- X2 moves away, first to create space in front, and then checks back
- X2 turns with the ball around the **OUTSIDE** of the cone
- X2 then passes to X3, and follows the pass
- X3 moves away and then checks in
- Repeat sequence

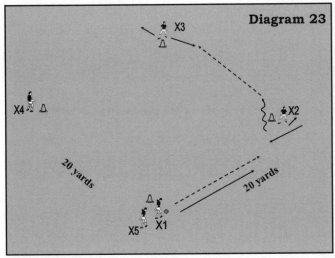

Diamond Drill Passing & Turning - Variation

Players must now turn to the **INSIDE** of cone before passing to next player in sequence.

X1 starts off with two touches to initiate X2 movement.

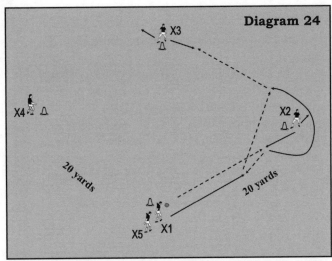

Diamond Drill - Passing, Setting & Spinning

- X1 plays off two touches to initiate X2 movement
- X1 passes to X2 and then creates angle
- X2 moves away to create space in front, checks back, sets ball to X1 and then spins around the cone to collect a "through" pass from X1
- X2 plays to X3, who has moved away and checked back. X2 moves inside to offer angle inside
- X3 sets for X2 and spins around cone
- X2 plays a "through" ball to X3
- Repeat sequence

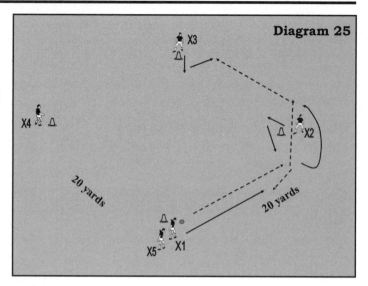

Diamond Drill - Passing, Setting & Spinning - Variation

Players must now move INSIDE of cone to create space outside.

Players spin to receive a "through" ball which has been played outside of the cone.

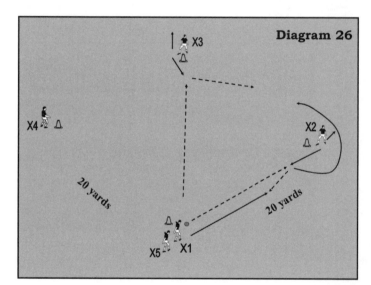

Diamond Drill - Passing, Setting & Spinning - Variation

- Players must now move away to create space in front
- X1 plays ball to X2 and supports inside
- X2 moves away to create space in front, then checks back to receive pass from X1
- X2 sets ball to X1 and then spins around outside of the cone
- X1 plays ball to target player X3
- X2 supports X3 with his outside run
- Repeat sequence using X3 as starting player and X5 as target player

Diamond Drill - Wall Pass Spinning & Turning

- X1 plays off two touches to initiate X2 and X4 movement
- X1 passes to X2 and follows pass
- X2 moves away to create space in front and then checks back. X2 plays ball into X4, who comes in short to play ball back behind X2's cone
- X2 spins behind and outside the cone and plays into X3
- Repeat sequence with X3 playing into X4 and X1 now offering the wall pass

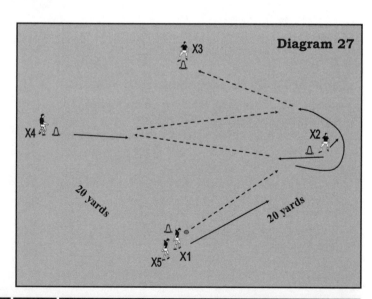

Diamond Drill - Progression

- X1 plays off two touches to initiate X2 and X4 movement
- X1 passes to X2 and moves inside for a support ball from X4
- X2 moves away to create space in front and then checks back to receive pass from X1
- X2 plays ball square to X4 who comes in short
- X2 spins behind and outside the cone and plays into X3
- X4 sets ball for X1, who in turn, slides ball inside of cone through to X2
- X2 passes to X3, who has moved away and checked in
- Repeat sequence in opposite direction

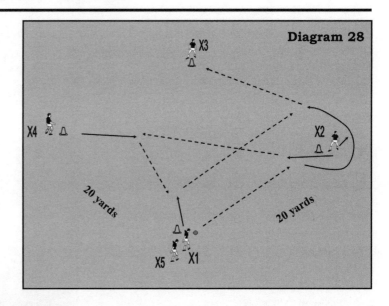

Diagram 28

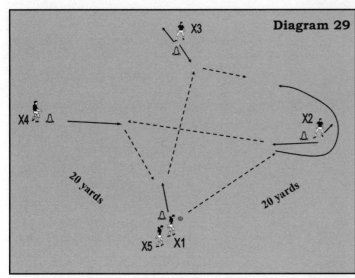

Diagram 29

Diamond Drill - Progression

- X1 plays off two touches to initiate X2 and X4 movement
- X1 passes to X2 and moves inside for a support ball from X4
- X2 moves away to create space in front and then checks back to receive pass from X1
- X2 plays ball square to X4 who comes in short
- X2 spins behind and outside the cone and plays into X3
- X4 sets ball for X1, who in turn plays up to target player X3
- X3 who has moved away and checked in, sets ball back to X2, who plays square pass to X4
- Repeat sequence in opposite direction

Diamond Drill - Crossing & Finishing

- X1 passes to X2 and moves inside for a support angle
- X2 moves away to create space in front and then checks back to receive pass from X1
- X2 sets ball back to X1, who plays ball to target X3
- X1 then overlaps X2
- X3 sets ball for X4 who in turn plays ball to X1
- X1 crosses ball to X3 and X4 who have made curving runs into the box
- X5 offers deeps support
- After completion of cross/finish, X5 become target player for the left side combination play
- Sequence is repeated on both sides

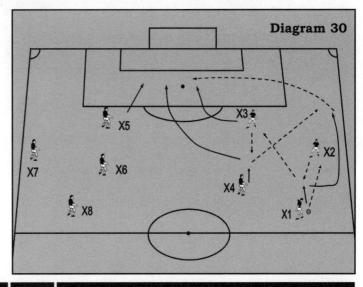

Diagram 30

Sheffield United Academy

This session was submitted by Kevin Fogg, Assistant Academy Director at Sheffield United Football Club.

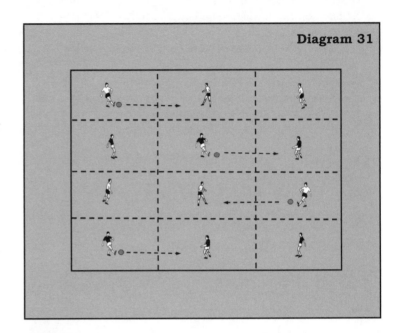

Diagram 31

Setting The Scene: Memories Through Quick Play Practices

A grid is set up with 12 squares inside and a player in each square. Play starts off with a ball in each grid line and the ball being passed up and down the line.

Variation

- Two ball set up - pass between
- One ball set up with one player to press the ball, but stay in own square

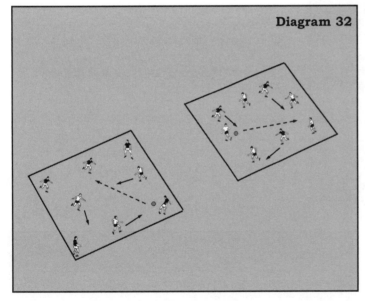

Diagram 32

Progression - Introduce Defenders

Play 5 v 3 keepaway in two grids. In one grid, the black team has the numerical advantage and in the other grid the white team has the numerical advantage.

Coaching Points

- Quick play movements
- Defenders should close down quickly and force turnovers

Playing Through The Midfield

The field is divided into thirds, with each end playing 3 v 2 and the middle third playing 3 v 3. Defenders outnumber the forwards 3 v 2 in their own defensive end.

The session begins with the goalkeeper playing the ball out to one of the back players. The objective for the defenders is to keep possession and play through the midfield whenever possible.

Once the ball has progressed to the middle third, the midfielders attempt to play the ball to the forwards. One player from the midfield can support the forwards and a defending midfielder can track this runner.

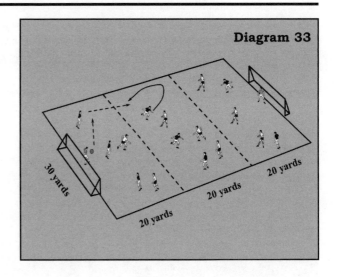

Diagram 33

Coaching Points
• Retain Balance
• Mix the play up. Pass and move or take people on

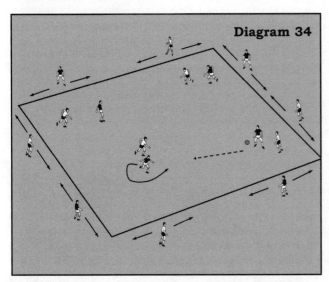

Diagram 34

Development of Practice - 4 v 4

This game plays 4 v 4 inside the grid, with each team having four supporting players on the outside.

Inside players have a two touch limit and those on the outside have one touch. Outside players to "work the line" and support play.

Players on the inside can exchange places with their team-mates on the outside, emptying and filling space.

Coaching Points
• Recognize movements
• Quality of movement, with and without the ball
• Communication with the outside players

Direction Game With Goalkeepers And Goals

The goalkeeper starts the session by throwing the ball to one of his defenders.

The two opposing defenders on the outside can come in and pressure once he has taken his first touch, creating a 4 v 2 situation.

Defenders play to create an opening to get the ball to their target players in the middle third. The target players combine to play the ball to their forwards in the offensive third.

Defenders again come in and close down to create a 4 v 3 situation. Repeat activity in the opposite direction.

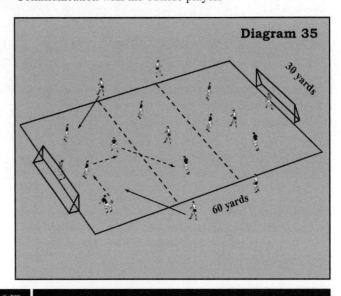

Diagram 35

England U17 National Team

This session is contributed by John Peacock, head coach of the England Under 17 National team. The session is helpful for teaching players to appreciate the quality of receiving and passing skills, which are allied to good support play. John Peacock is the featured clinician at our International Coaching Seminar in Omaha, December 10 - 12.

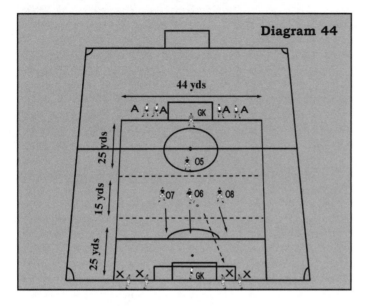

Organization

Three teams of four or three teams of five, plus two goalkeepers. Vary the dimensions of field depending on squad size and quality of players.

O6 plays the ball into any of the X players creating a 3 v 4 situation. Players to remain in the third with the objective of getting one player out to attack O5 on 1 v 1. O5 can't come off this start position until an X player gets over the line. Repeat practice the other way.

Progressions

- An extra X player joins in to create a 2 v 1 situation
- If O5 wins the ball, O's quickly counter attack the X players

Coaching Points

- X players spread out to become difficult to mark
- Look to work the opening by moving the ball quickly and switching play
- Once out, speed of attack - techniques, running with the ball, dribbling and finishing
- Support positions, i.e. movement off the ball to create space

Receiving The Ball "In The Hole" In Order To Attack

GK throws to either X5 or X6. O9 and O10 can close down after first touch. X5 can either play forward to X9 or X10, or play wide to X2 or X3, who have two touches to play forward. X2 and X3 cannot be challenged. One attacker, X9 or X10, can come into shaded area to receive unopposed. Combine with X10 to finish (2 v 2). Repeat other way.

Develop by allowing X5 or X6 to make forward runs into attacking half when the ball goes into X9 or X10, therefore creating 3 v 2 situation. As that is happening, X2 or X3 drops into central area to keep 2 v 2 at back. X5 then drops out to the side lines if X2 went in as the defender.

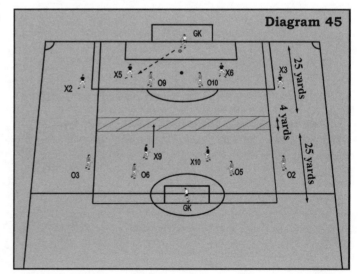

Coaching Points

- Play forward - quality and selection of pass
- Receiving qualities of the attacker in the shaded area
- Combination of play in the attacking half. Also in 3 v 2, timing and speed of supporting run

Golden Goal

This goal was scored by Lee Chapman for Leeds United in a game against Sheffield Wednesday during the 1991 - 1992 season. It highlights how quick distribution from the goalkeeper can lead to quick counter-attacking goal chances. The build-up included a throw from the goalkeeper, followed by one pass and a cross for a headed goal and took six seconds.

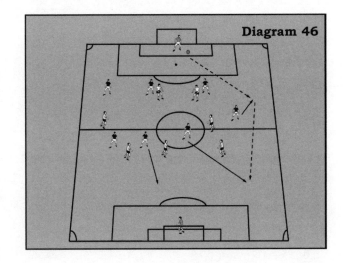

The goalkeeper, John Lukic, starts with the ball and throws wide to the left back, Tony Dorigo, who drops back to get open for the pass.

Dorigo allows the ball to run across his body and then hits a one-touch pass into the space for the running Gary Speed.

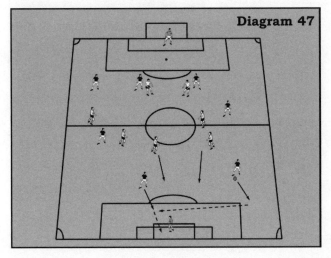

Gary Speed takes one touch into space and then hits a cross for the incoming Lee Chapman to head into goal from 10 yards out.

Manchester United

Contributed by Kenichi Yatsuhashi from BMCC Athletics, Men's soccer. Kenichi is an Eastern New York Youth Soccer Association Staff Coach. The session was observed at Giants Stadium on July 30th, 2004. Manchester United was due to play AC Milan the next day.

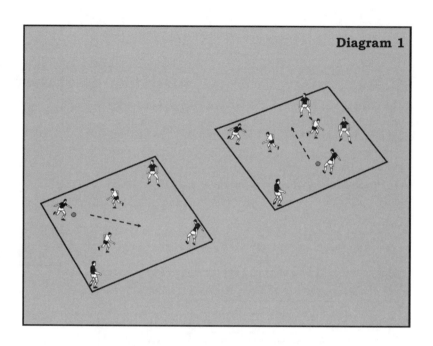

Warm-Up

The players arrive shortly after the coaches and begin a warm-up consisting of two gentle slow paced laps of the field. After the team finishes the two laps, three goalkeepers start working with the goalkeeper coach while the field players stretch both statically and dynamically. After the players conclude the stretching, they again jog around the field twice.

Players divide into small groups and play 4 v 2 or 5 v 2 keep-away.

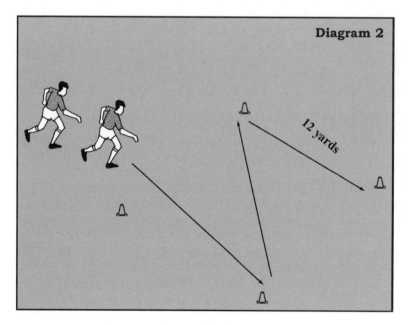

Goalkeeping Exercises

The goalkeepers continue working without a ball by performing some fast feet shuttle runs, zigzagging throughout cones. They conclude with some dynamic stretching and some ball juggling activities.

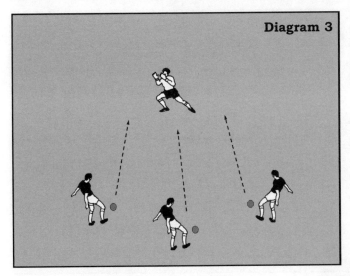

Diagram 3

Goalkeeping Exercises Cont'd

The goalkeepers begin working on their handling skills. One goalkeeper works, while the coach and the other two goalkeepers take turns serving balls to the working goalkeeper. Each goalkeeper performs a desired number of catches and saves, then rotates with the other goalkeepers. Balls are mainly served at head height.

Goalkeeping Exercises Cont'd

Goalkeepers progress to working on their diving skills. In a 4 x 4-yard area, one goalkeeper works while the other two serve balls down each side of square. The working goalkeeper performs six saves and then rests.

Coaching Point

- Goalkeepers must "set" themselves before diving
- Goalkeepers must use correct footwork technique, moving from side to side

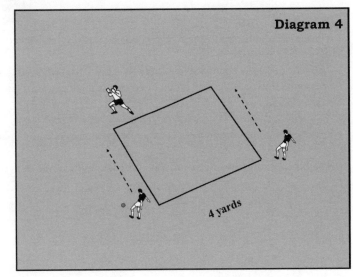

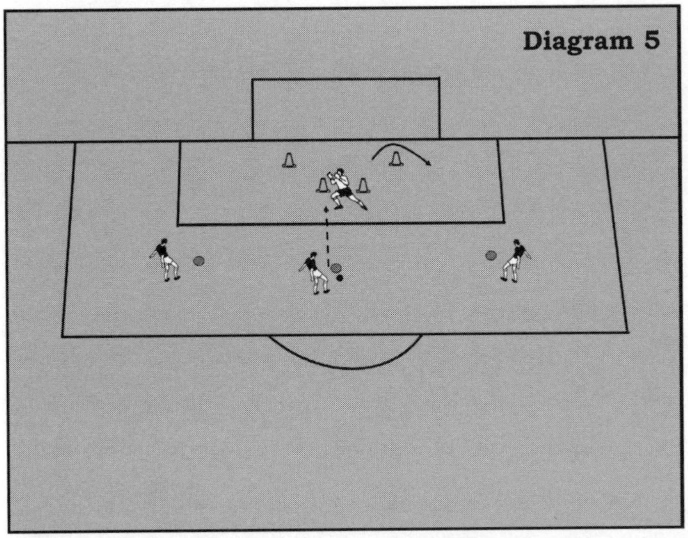

Diagram 4

4 yards

Goalkeeping Exercises Cont'd

The goalkeeper coach stands on the penalty spot with non-working goalkeepers. They are level with him, but at 45 degrees to goal.

Two cones are positioned four yards from goal line with two other cones positioned diagonally behind. These cones are to represent where the goalkeeper should "set" himself prior to making a save.

Once he has made the initial save from the goalkeeper coach, the goalkeeper backs up around one of the other cones to make a save to that side.

Variations

Vary the height of each service.

Diagram 5

Manchester United

Final Theme

Teams are divided up and players positioned in the following manner:

- White team plays with three defensive backs, two holding midfielders, two wide wingers and two forwards
- Black team plays with four defensive backs, one midfielder and three forwards

Players are told to stay in their respective positions to create the following scenarios:

- 3 v 3 in one defensive third
- 4 v 1 in middle third
- 4 v 2 in one defensive third

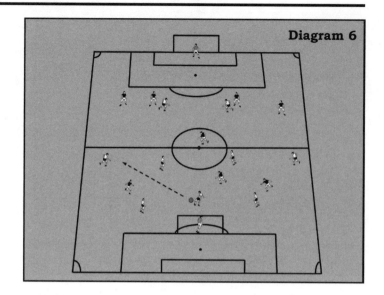

Diagram 6

Coaching Points

- These restrictions are to encourage counter-attacking and speed of play

- The black team is conditioned to play long balls from their defensive end and "bypass" the midfield. The white team is encouraged to pass the ball around and use midfielders as much as possible (because of their numerical advantage 4 v 1)

- Coaches intervene whenever necessary to give guidance and "paint a picture" of what should happen

- The black team forwards are told to stay high up field and then one is to check in and receive pass

Manchester United Symposium

Ozzie White, DOC of Ankeny Soccer Club attended the Euro Sportring/Manchester United Symposium in Chicago, conducted in conjunction with their Champions Tour games this summer, and shares his experience.

As a lifelong Manchester United fan I could not wait for the day when the team would play in America. I promised my American wife and two children that wherever the games were played, we would attend. Double bonus, United versus Celtic, the other team I have followed all my life. We had a magical time last year in Seattle and my son was hooked.

A year later and United are returning to the States. How can we top the experience from last year? We can attend two games!! My wife was suspicious, but to Jake (son) and me, it was the perfect logic.

Man Utd. Versus Bayern Munich in Chicago, followed by United and Celtic in Philadelphia. The perfect summer vacation!

I then read about the coaching Symposium presented by Renee Mulensteen, the United Skills Coach, in my issue of WORLDCLASSCOACHING. The symposium was based on United's philosophy of player development. How could I miss such an event?

I took a friend from the Urbandale Soccer Club, John Amato. We arrived excited about the symposium and the game to follow. On the way into the lecture room we were met and greeted by one of the games greatest ever players, Sir Bobby Charlton. A pleasure and an honor to meet the record goal scorer for England, and a true United legend.

Sir Bobby gave the crowd a selection of stories from his vast repertoire, before introducing Renee Mulensteen, a Dutchman who has revolutionized United's approach to player development. Mulensteen works with all players, from the starry eyed hopefuls, to the first team players. Mulensteen started with a general discussion and then moved into a high tech power point presentation which I interpreted like this:

You research the history of the player. You analyze the social and economic background, you look at the cultural background and also the experiences the player has had. The reference point should be, "what makes the difference in the game?"

Analyze the world's most successful teams and see who they are: Brazil, Germany, Argentina, Italy, France, and England.

All of these are winners of the World Cup within the last 40 years. Which teams have won the Champions League over the last 20 years and why? What are the qualities of these successful teams? (Best players, hard work, team work, game plan, winning mentality, score goals.)

Who are the players, why are they the best, what qualities do they bring to the winning teams? Players such as Charlton, Pele, Cruyff, Beckenbuer, Maradona, Zidane, Ronaldo, Maldini all have great skills, but they offer a mentality above the average player that drives teammates to the next level. All of the great players have something in common. They can dominate the 1 versus 1 situation, either defensively or offensively.

All of the great teams can also dominate the 1 v 1 situation.

- Defensively through their shape
- Ability to win tackles or intercept
- Quickness to the second ball
- Ability to defend set pieces and gain possession

Offensively the successful teams win through:

- Shape and position (tactics)
- The ability to change the play (disguise)
- Change pace (speed of play)
- Change direction with the ball (switch the point of attack)
- Change direction without the ball (unbalance)
- Ability to score from set pieces

All of these attacking qualities are unpredictable to the defending team.

Manchester United's template for the world class player is broken down into a jigsaw of attacking qualities and defensive qualities. They also use the four pillars of the game to divide the qualities into recognizable moments in the game.

Physically - The players must be match fit and have match pace. Can they adapt to the speed of play, can they dictate the momentum of the game?

> **"Allow them to play kids games with kid's rules and kids results. The coach just sets up the environment, and then shuts up."**

Technically - Can the players perform moves, turns, tricks, can they tackle, pass, and dribble? Essentially, what is the skill level of the player?

Tactically - Does the player understand the game, the plan, the shape? What decision making skills does the player have?

Mentally - Is the player tough enough to survive at the top level? What personality does the player possess? Is the player a natural winner, or fighter, or does the player quit when the going gets a little rough?

Renee then made a statement which I did not need to write down to remember. It is a quote which impacted me as a coach and certainly made me reflect on my training sessions.

"DEVELOPMENT IS THE RIGHT EMPHASIS AT THE RIGHT TIME."

He went on to add that "EVERYTHING IS INTER-RELATED."

The whole game revolves around the 1 versus 1 situation. Good players are adept at beating opponents. Good teams contain more players adept at 1 v 1 than their opponents. The game comprises of many 1 v 1 battles around the pitch, if your team wins the majority, then you stand a good chance of winning the game.

Renee stated there are four components to the 1 v 1 situation;
• Side
• Front
• Back
• Side

A player must develop all four areas to enhance the ability to win in the 1 v 1 contest.

Renee uses a simple name to emphasize his philosophy on player development - TED.

T – Talent   E – Enthusiasm   D – Determination

The audience then watched a couple of segments from Manchester United's developmental DVD; *"Play like*

Champions". It is exciting to see the youngsters get opportunities to learn from and watch their heroes in this production. Renee ended his fine presentation with another philosophical quote which is a good one to make parents and spectators aware of;

"ALLOW THEM TO PLAY KIDS GAMES WITH KID'S RULES AND KIDS RESULTS. THE COACH JUST SETS UP THE ENVIRONMENT, AND THEN SHUTS UP."

The symposium was a very worthwhile event. It gave me a new outlook in some aspects of the game and helped reinforce some of my own methods and philosophies. It is nice to know that my philosophies are not a million miles away from a club with the pedigree of Manchester United. It is also refreshing to understand that player development is not rocket science in theory. If you stick to the principles of the game, set up the right problem solving environment, be patient and allow the players to express themselves without fear of failure, I believe you have done your part for your players.

Upon completion of the Seminar we were ushered upstairs to join the sell out crowd and for me to sit with my son and revert to being just a Man Utd. fan again. The game is not for me to analyze, but it was not the classic we all wanted. Oh well, nothing will quell my passion and enthusiasm for what is "by far the greatest team the world has ever seen".

It would be remiss of me not to quote the man who has taken Manchester United to unsurpassed levels of excellence, Sir Alex Ferguson.

"IF YOU HAVE A DREAM, YOU BETTER HAVE A BIG ONE."

My wife has already asked if Manchester United is coming back next year. Well, they are touring Australia!!! Anyone know a good travel agent?

> **"The whole game revolves around the 1 versus 1 situation. Good players are adept at beating opponents. Good teams contain more players adept at 1 v 1 than their opponents"**

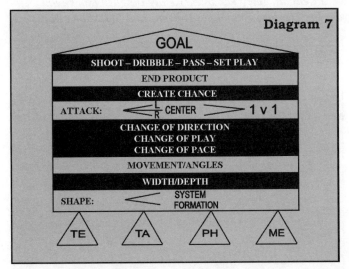

Diagram 7

The symposium can be encapsulated with this diagram, referred to as the "Developmental Rocket":

- The bottom of the rocket (engines) illustrates the four pillars of the game; Technical, Tactical, Physical, and Psychological.
- The first stage is the foundation of the tactics – the shape or formation.
- Width and Depth provide movement and angles.
- Unpredictability is a change of direction, pace, or switch in play.
- The attack comes from the left, right, or middle, making the most of 1 v 1 situations.
- The team creates chances from successful 1 v 1's.
- What is the end product? Shoot, dribble, pass, or a set play. GOALS!!

Goals are the ultimate aim, the point of the rocket and the passport to success.

Bobby Mimms - Goalkeeping

Bobby Mimms, currently the first team goalkeeper coach at Wolverhampton Wanderers, submits these goalkeeper practices. Mimms has played under managers such as Howard Kendall, Terry Venables, Kenny Dalglish and Glenn Hoddle. He has over 550 league and cup appearances playing for Everton, Tottenham Hotspur and Blackburn Rovers.

Warm-Up

Goalkeepers warm up with a gentle jog and some stretching. The intensity is increased with some fast footwork exercises.

Goalkeepers line up behind a series of cones and perform various movements around and over the markers.
- High knees
- Heel flicks
- Zig-Zag
- Side-Shuffles
- Cross-overs

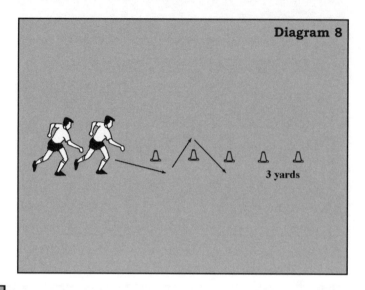

Ball Handling

Server volleys and half-volleys 12 times to goalkeepers, varying the height and pace of service.

Coaching Points
- Get in line with the ball quickly
- Correct handling technique - W formation
- Bring ball into chest after making save

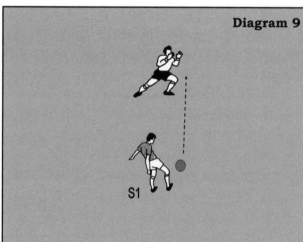

Reaction Saves - Turning Off The Post

Server lines up six yards out from goal line and slightly off center. Goalkeeper lines up on the post facing outwards. On coaches command, goalkeeper spins inside and makes save from server.

Coaching Points
- Get in line with the ball quickly
- Shuffle across the line - heels clicking
- Server to volley and half volley

Progression(s)
- Work keeper by moving closer and further away
- Work from both sides
- Make goalkeeper line up at furthest post away

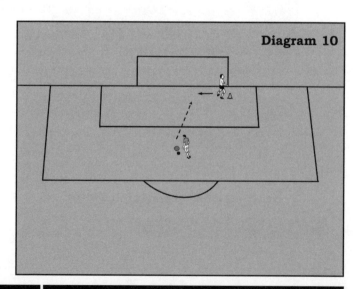

Bobby Mimms - Goalkeeping

Reaction Saves - Movement Into Post

Server lines up as before, but with goalkeeper now directly in front. On command from coach, the goalkeeper shuffles to near post, touching it, then reacts to servers shot and saves.

Coaching Points
- Get in line with the ball quickly
- Shuffle across the line - heels clicking
- Collapse on ball to prevent rebounds
- Server to volley and half volley
- Allow server to choose type of service

Progression(s)
- Work keeper by moving closer and further away
- Work from both sides

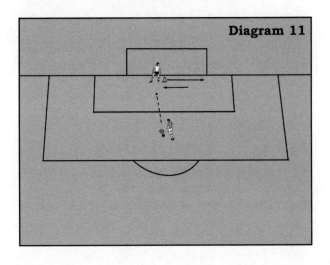
Diagram 11

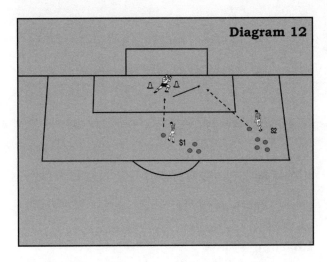
Diagram 12

Recovery Saves

Two servers line up as shown, with goalkeeper now directly in front of S1, in between two markers. Goalkeeper makes save from S1, then moves into line to make save from S2.

Coaching Points
- Get in "ready" position - up on toes and hands ready
- Make initial save and bounce up quickly
- S2 to shoot quickly after S1
- Vary type and pace of service

Progression(s)
- Have servers dribble prior to shooting
- Work from both sides
- Start with S2 first

Recovery Saves

Two servers line up side by side with the goalkeeper lying down near one of the posts. On the coaches command, the servers play balls for goalkeeper to save. S1 throws a ball into top corner. S2 side foots a ball low on ground.

Coaching Points
- Bounce up quickly and react to shots
- Two fast saves - work the goalkeeper hard
- S2 to shoot quickly after S1
- Vary type and pace of service
- Give goalkeeper realistic chance of making saves

Progression(s)
- Work from both sides
- Move in closer or further away, depending on goalkeepers ability to react

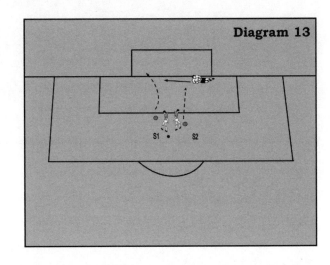
Diagram 13

Working Down The Line

S1 approaches the goal at a 45 degree angle, coming in from the edge of the box. Goalkeeper takes position accordingly to "narrow the angle", coming forward from line and makes the save. Once the save has been made, recover back to starting position indicated by the cone. The server also returns to the edge of the box.

Coaching Points

- Get in line with the ball quickly
- Shuffle across the line - heels clicking
- Set yourself prior to shot

Progression(s)

- Work keeper by moving closer and further away
- Attack goal from both sides
- Make goalkeeper lie, sit down, then bounce up and move into position

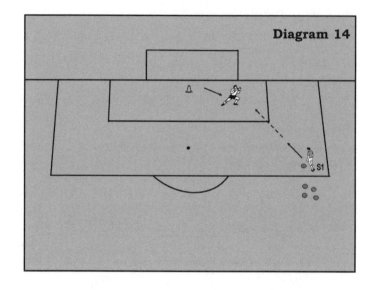

Diagram 14

Working Down The Line With Recovery

This is a continuation of the previous exercise with a second server waiting at the penalty spot. Once the goalkeeper has made his initial save, he recovers quickly to make a second save from the second server. After making his two saves he recovers to his starting position indicated by the cone.

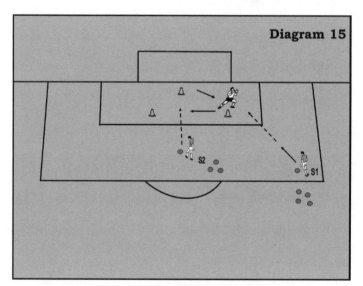

Diagram 15

Coaching Points

- Get in line with the ball quickly - ready position - on toes and hands up ready
- Shuffle across the line - heels clicking
- Bounce up quickly after first save
- Set yourself prior to shot

Progression(s)

- Work keeper by moving closer and further away
- Attack goal from both sides

Bobby Mimms - Goalkeeping

Fast Footwork and Save

Here, the goalkeeper starts at one end of the cones and performs a series of footwork exercises through them before making a save from the server.

- Zig-zag runs
- Two-foot jumps
- Shuffles

Coaching Points

- Concentrate on footwork
- Get in ready position early, and set yourself
- Look ahead as you go through the cones

Progression(s)

- Work keeper by moving closer and further away
- Attack goal from both sides

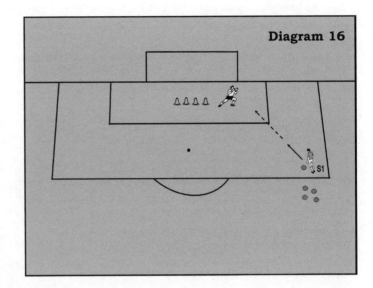

Diagram 16

Working Down The Line

The goalkeeper starts in the middle of the goal and rushes quickly around the cone before making a diving save to his left.

The exercise is repeated on the other side of the goal so that the keeper makes a diving save to his right.

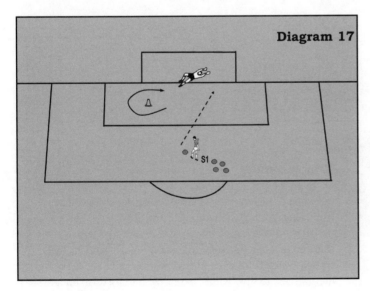

Diagram 17

Coaching Points

- Concentrate on footwork - don't cross over feet
- The server waits until the keeper is around the cone before taking shot
- Server aims away from diving goalkeeper

Progression(s)

- Work keeper by moving closer and further away
- Add a second server to make the goalkeeper work harder - run around cone, make save, get up, run around cone, make second save

Crystal Palace Academy

This session is submitted by Derek Broadley, former Academy Director with Crystal Palace F.C. and Murray Jones, who is the Assistant Academy Director for 16-21 year olds at Crystal Palace Football Club. Broadley is now the National Director of Coaching for Premier Skills, a coach education company and is also President of www.soccer-expert.com.

Developing Play From The Back

The practice starts with a 7 v 5 situation and a GK using two thirds of the pitch. The practice is slightly overloaded to allow the back players the opportunity to be successful and gain confidence. We encourage them to understand the aims of the session and to perform the relevant skills repetitively.

The black fullbacks run and receive possession in wide areas, (place visual cues, colored gates) creating opportunities for central defenders to carry ball out and transfer possession into forward or attacking fullback areas or to play into midfield players.

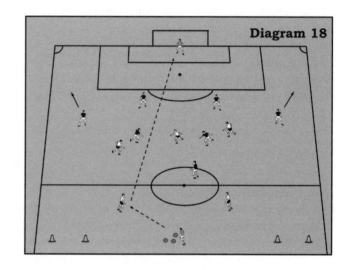

Develop possession and ball retention skills in deep areas for all players. Encourage midfield players to receive and develop possession.

Whites attempt to regain possession to:
• Chip into Gk
• Win possession and score

Blacks to get the ball under control, through the end gates.

Coaching Points
• Defenders to take playing and positional cues off delivery into GK
• Encourage fullbacks to receive high and wide
• Develop a situation to transfer and switch possession across the back
• Ability of central defenders to play and travel with the ball out of defending areas
• Confidence of back players to develop the game

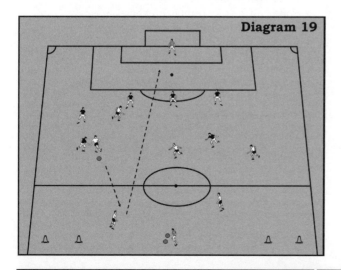

Progression(s)

Develop the practice into a 6 v 6, 7 v 7, etc. situation, with the same organization and similar starting points. The blacks can now receive a pass or travel with the ball into the 10-yard target area that is beyond the half line. As the practice now begins to flourish, continually address the technical needs for each player, while again, encouraging the fullback to give width and move into forward areas. The whites can now score on regaining possession. When the GK is under pressure, encourage him to play a long pass into the coach in a central position, who can then restart the practice.

Training Overlaps

The following series of drills focusing on overlaps are presented by Wayne Harrison Director of Player and Coach Development for Eden Prairie Soccer Club in Minnesota. Harrison is also the author of a number of best-selling coaching books. This is Part One of a two part series. Part Two will appear in the March/April issue.

- Once the technique of overlapping is established, bring a competitive element into each session and each set-up.
- Count the number of overlaps each player can perform successfully in a given time period.
- Have them compete against themselves first, so with each session they get a number of chances to beat their own previous score over the same time period and over the same distance.
- Then they can compete against each other, ensure the players are at a similar level of ability when you do this so no one is left embarrassed by their score.
- In the 3 v 1 or 3 v 2 set-ups have it as a team competition, each team gets to have 10 attacks on goal for example, and count which team has the most shots or headers on target, or ultimately scores the most goals.

(1) Runs with the ball and plays a give-and-go with (6), then lays the ball off to (5). At the same time (6) makes an overlap run around (5) to receive the pass in front. (1) takes the place of (6).

The support run is in the form of an overlap.

Timing of the overlap run is important, as is the timing of the pass into space in front of the overlapping player to receive. Introduce more players with a ball each to develop the session.

An awareness is required of each player performing the overlap run and taking the ball, of where these other players are and where they are going to. This applies to all the overlapping set ups so the A.I.A. principles (Anticipation - Imagination - Awareness) are practiced to great effect here in the various phases of overlapping play.

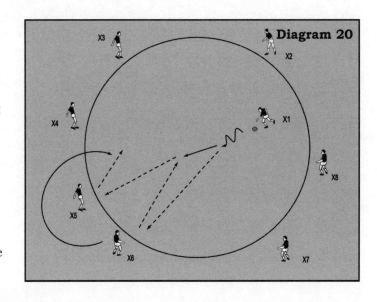

Diagram 20

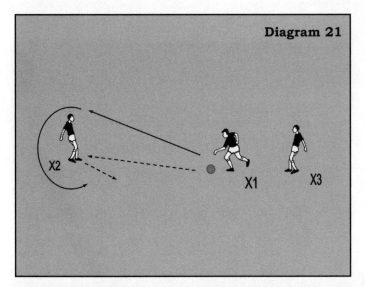

Diagram 21

Continuous movements making overlapping runs with two players either side. (1) passes to (2) and overlaps, (2) passes into the path of (1)'s run and (1) then runs with the ball and passes to (3) and overlaps, and the circuit continues.

Rotate the players after a number of moves each.

Coach calls switch and the players can change as the movement is going on. This is an easy way to establish overlapping and making it work on a consistent basis with no opposition.

On each set-up, make it competitive where the players count the number of overlaps they get done in a set time.

Training Overlaps

Progression(s)

Now making diagonal runs across the field to opposite players, for example (1) and (4) have to be aware of each others position, as well as doing the overlap, which is an extension of A.I.A. training also.

(1) works with (2) and (3). (4) works with (5) and (6).

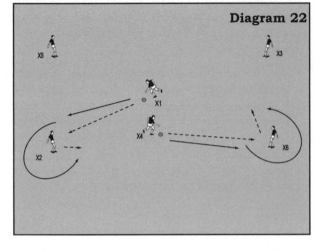

Diagram 22

Divide the players into two teams. One team of players inside the circle with a ball each, and one team on the outside to help effect the overlap.

For example player (7) passes to player (5) who brings the ball across and inside to create space outside for the overlapping player.

(7) overlaps (5) and receives the pass into his path back from (5) to continue linking up with the other players and effecting the overlap situations.

Communication from the passing player is necessary, it can be "hold" for the receiving player to know they need to keep control until the player is ready to receive the ball back after the overlap has been completed.

Coach calls "switch", and the inside players switch with the outside players, and the theme is continued without stopping.

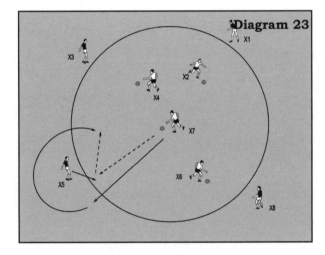

Diagram 23

Now open it up so everyone is in the circle.

Have players working in two's (one from each team if you like) moving freely around the area implementing the overlap technique.

After one player has worked for a while, call "switch" and change roles.

This is more difficult for the players because everyone is moving and they must decide the time to work the overlap more carefully. Emphasize the sequence again: pass to the receiver, communication, open the space up with one touch, player overlaps, pass into the path of the overlapping player.

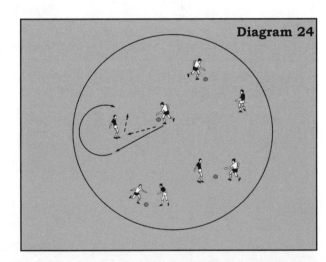

Diagram 24

Training Overlaps

Progression(s)

Develop the idea and have players now passing to any player on the other team without a ball, not working, in specific pairs anymore. More awareness of where players are and who is free, is needed now and this aids the players peripheral vision as well as improving their overlapping ability.

As previously done, call "switch", and the players without the ball receive it, and the players with the ball now become the receivers to engineer the overlap. This ensures the session continues without a break or a stop.

With there being more players in the immediate area, there is less space to work in so the pass back from the receiver to the overlapping player has to be precise, well timed and properly weighted, so the overlapping players do not have to break stride to receive the pass back. Otherwise, make the area they are playing in a larger area if you are having trouble with the spacing.

Coaching Points

- Create Space – Receiver brings the ball inside to create space outside for the overlapping player, particularly in a wide area of the field
- Communication – Overlapping player calls "HOLD"
- Timing of the run – When the receiving player is faced forward
- Angle of the run – Wide away from the defender
- Timing of the pass – Into the path in front of the overlapping player with correct weight so the overlapping player does not have to break stride
- Decoy or pass – Instead of passing, use the run to take a defender away from the space inside and come inside with the ball

Attacking the goal from the edge of the penalty area, two attackers take on one defender and a goalkeeper. X1 cuts inside and dribbles toward the defender. X2 overlaps X1. X1 plays the ball into X2's path. X2 attempts to beat the goalkeeper.

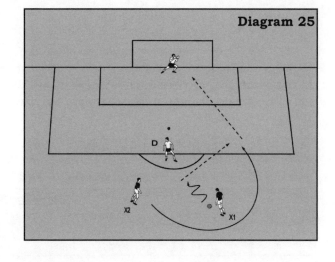

Diagram 25

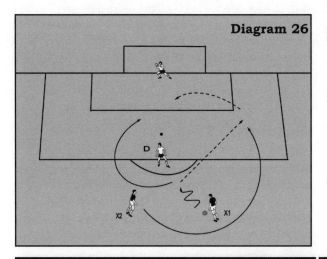

Diagram 26

Same set up as previous, but now, once X2 has overlapped, X1 plays the ball down the line for X2 to cross. After X1 has passed the ball down the line, he runs into the goal area to score from the cross.

Progression

Add a second defender making it 2 v 2.

Training Overlaps

With this overload situation it is a very good opportunity to practice overlaps, give-and-go's, diagonal runs in front of the ball and takeovers.

(A) or (B) pass the ball into any of the three attackers and close them down as the ball travels. Try to create a 2 v 1 set-up somewhere on the field of play from the 3 v 2 situation. If it proves difficult to set up and execute successfully, start with a 3 v 1 situation and then go to a 3 v 2 when it starts to work regularly.

Players can make their plays using each others movement as a decoy, as well as an exchange of possession of the ball.

Playing offside makes this set-up more realistic.

Condition the attacking players so they can only score with two touches (or only one touch if possible).

This set-up shows a typical overlap situation. (1) can make two decisions: to pass to (2) and overlap or use (2)'s run to take (B) out of position and come inside with the ball creating a 2 v 1 against (A).

It is important for players to realize, in this case (2), that they make runs to create space for themselves and also for their teammates.

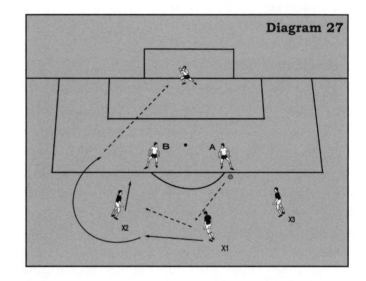
Diagram 27

With this overlap situation it is a very good opportunity to practice overlaps. (A) and (B) pass the ball into any of the three attackers and close them down as the ball travels. Try to create a 2 v 1 set up somewhere on the field of play from the 3 v 2 situation. Players can make their plays using each others movement as a decoy as well as an exchange of possession of the ball.

Playing offside makes this set up more realistic.

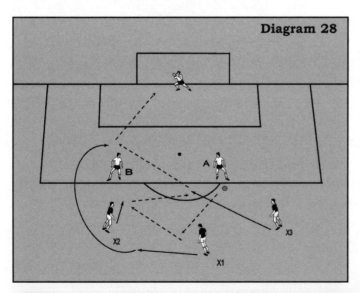
Diagram 28

This set-up shows a typical overlap situation. (2) can make the following decisions when he receives the ball: to pass directly to (1) on the overlap or use (1's) run to take (B) out of position and come inside with the ball creating a 2 v 1 against (A). Perhaps effect an overlap here too against (B) !!

It is important for the players to realize (in this case player 1) that they make runs to create space for themselves and also for their teammates.

Another option, as shown here, is to work with (3) to make the pass to overlapping player (1). There are various ways to achieve your goal in this 3 v 2.

Introduce keepers if you have them available. If defenders win the ball they can score as a reward.

Training Overlaps

Progression(s)

Introduce keepers and increase the size of the goals to make the set up more realistic. You can also have keepers in from the beginning if you wish.

With more numbers, have the players rotate on and off in 3 v 2 situations. You may need to make a 4 v 2 situation depending on the ability of the players.

You can show them tried and tested ways to create overload situations (as previously shown) to begin, then let it go free and see them use their own imagination.

Rotate players so defenders get the chance to be attackers and attackers to be defenders. Rotate keepers.

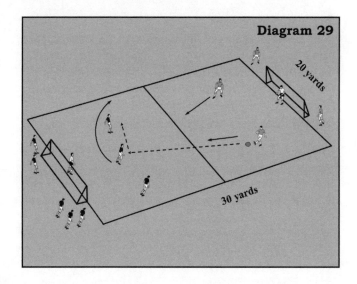

Diagram 29

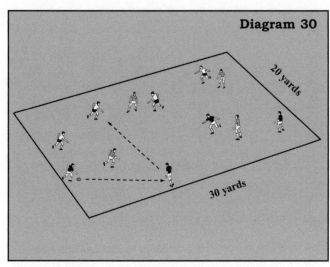

Diagram 30

Teams (1) and (2) work together to keep the ball from team (3). If team (3) regains possession, the team who gave it away become the defenders. The defenders reward is they now keep the ball and link with the other team.

Rules: Once possession is gained, to establish who gave the ball away, the defender who won the ball puts their foot on the ball to stop play and the coach can call out the team who gave it away. Play begins again working on transitions.

Progression(s)

Increase difficulty for attackers by:

• Reducing the zone size
• Decreasing the number of touches on the ball of each player.
• Condition the passing to be only to the other attacking teams players, e.g. (1) only pass to (2) and vice versa, therefore only half the number of passes available per player
• You can increase the numbers to suit how many players you have, e.g. 4 v 4 v 4 or 5 v 5 v 5 etc.

Change the game to 6 v 3, staying the same time limit. Count the number of goals they score by doing overlaps, then have another 6 v 3. Every time a successful overlap is performed, the team gets a goal. See which combination of teams score the most goals by performing the most overlaps.

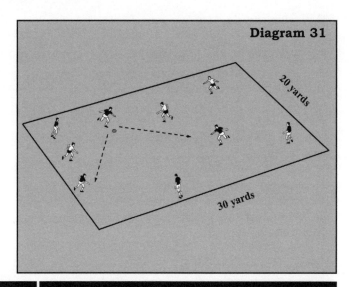

Diagram 31

Training Overlaps

This is a game situation developing the overlapping theme using simple examples of overlap runs in a 4 v 4 game. For simplicity and to ensure overlaps are practiced, from throw-ins or goal kicks, set the condition that the opposition can't move until a non-competitive overlap has been performed. Once this has been done, and the overlapping player has received the ball, the opponents can begin to play.

Every time a player passes the ball forward in the game, they must perform an overlap move with the receiver. This shows a pass and overlap run from (3) working with receiver (4) who brings the ball inside to create more space outside for the run of (3).

If successfully performed in a wide area (where most overlaps will occur), then in this example, (2) is now making a run into space to receive the cross.

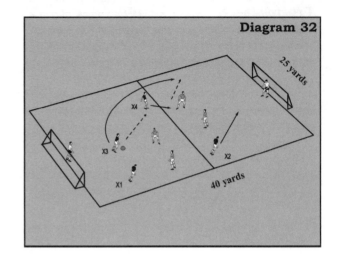

Diagram 32

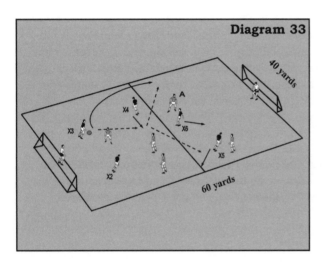

Diagram 33

Taking the overlapping game into a 6 v 6 situation, which is pertinent to U9's, we have an example of a back player (3) working with a midfield player (4), performing an overlap in a wide area of the field.

(4) brings the ball inside to clear the space for (3), who is making the overlapping run, note also: striker (6) moving inside to clear the space in front of (3) taking the defender (A) away also. (3) can now continue the run forward with the ball into space to get into a likely crossing position.

If (A) were to stay in the space to try to stop the forward run of (3), then (6) is available to receive a pass inside from (3).

Now take it into an 8 v 8 game, the set-up pertinent for U10's.

Here is an example of a throw-in situation where the uncontested overlap to begin the game is shown.

You could argue this is an "under-lap" because it is coming inside, but it is still technically passing and overlapping the receiver.

Of course the "when" and "where" of overlapping is important, and this must be emphasized and taught, but we just want to get the players performing overlap movements to begin with.

Continued in the next issue...

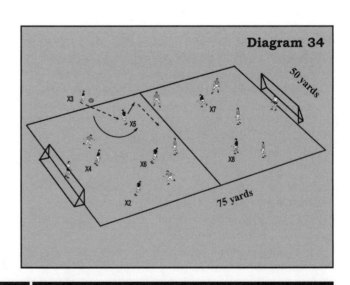

Diagram 34

Golden Goal

This goal was scored by Steve McManaman for England in a game against Portugal at the Euro 2000 Championships. The build up shows the benefits of having a player capable of long throws. In this instance, the build up starts with a long throw from his own half down the flank from Gary Neville to a running Michael Owen.

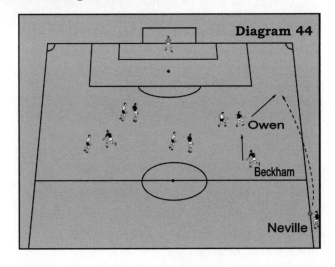

Gary Neville takes a long throw down the flank. Michael Owen makes a run into space to get on the end of the throw.

Owen, pressured by a defender, turns back and away from goal and makes a sideways pass inside for David Beckham.

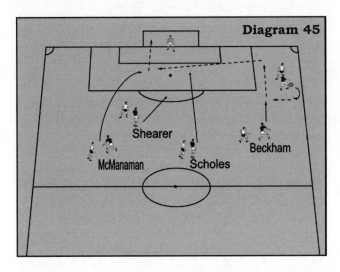

As the throw is taking place, Scholes, whose starting position is just inside the attacking half, starts a run toward the near post. Shearer, whose starting position is further forward, delays his run to arrive in the penalty area after Scholes. McManaman curves his run to arrive late at the far post.

When he receives the pass, Beckham pushes the ball with one touch into the space ahead of him and crosses a high ball toward the far post. McManaman arrives unmarked and side foots the ball in the goal with one touch.

Rangers F.C. Academy

This session is contributed by Andy Gould, Senior Community Coach at Rangers F.C. Andy is in charge of the Rangers Soccer Schools programs that include Residential Camps for teams and individuals; Andy has previously worked as a Regional Development Manager with the Scottish Football Association. The session focuses on the step-over move to beat an opponent. Each session follows a standard format with the addition of speed and agility training.

Warm-Up Touch & Technique

Within a 20 x 30-yard area, players dribble freely. On coaches command, execute a step-over or any other conditioned movements (using alternate feet; inside-inside, outside-outside, sole of foot, front of foot, change of direction every four touches) with the ball.

Coaching Points

- Balance
- Awareness
- Change of direction
- Change of pace

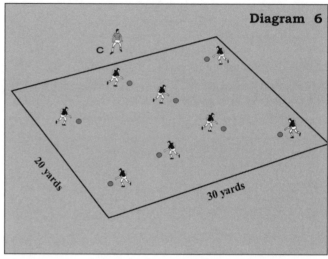

Step-Over In Pairs

In pairs, players with a ball each face each other 20 yards apart. On the coaches signal, dribble towards partner and in the middle execute a step-over move to left or right and dribble through to opposite end. Ensure players' work on both left and right step-over.

Coaching Points

- Awareness of opponent
- Timing of execution
- Create disguise with step-over low over ball and dip shoulder
- Touch wide of defender with outside of foot
- Change of pace

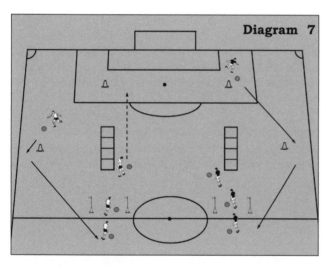

Speed & Agility (Incorporating ball)

In small groups, the players execute a series of fast feet and agility exercises incorporating a ball. At the starting point, play a pass to the end of the ladder, execute a two-step run through the ladders, retrieve the pass and return to start point executing a step-over at the marker. A variety of agility exercise can be introduced here along with various conditioned moves with the ball.

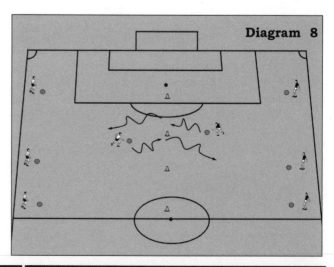

Rangers F.C. Academy

Game Related Activity – Step-Over & Shoot

Two groups situated at right hand side of each goal 40 yards apart. On the coaches signal, players at either goal dribble to center and execute step-over to right then shoot at goal. After shooting, each player joins opposite group.

Coaching Points

- Awareness of opponent
- Timing of execution
- Create disguise with step-over low over ball and dip shoulder
- Touch wide of defender with outside of foot
- Change of pace
- Aim for corner of goal

Progression(s)

- Introduce passive defenders
- Without goalkeepers, encourage players to hit the corner of the goal utilizing markers

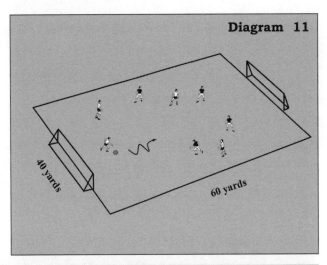

Diagram 9

40 yards

Conditioned Game 1 v 1

Games are played on a 40 x 30-yard grid with goals at one end of the field. Defender/attacker start at side of goal area. Defender feeds ball over attackers head into dead space for attacker to retrieve. As attacker approaches ball defender attempts to close down. Attackers are encouraged to execute step-over move to beat opponent before scoring. If defender wins possession, roles are changed.

Coaching Points

- Awareness of opponent
- Timing of execution
- Create disguise with step-over low over ball and dip shoulder
- Touch wide of defender with outside of foot
- Change of pace
- Aim for corner of goal

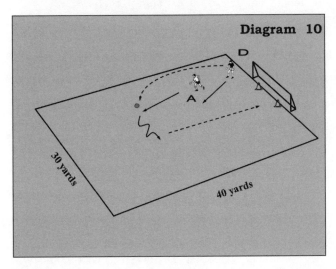

Diagram 10

D

A

30 yards

40 yards

Small-Sided Game 4 v 4

Two teams of four play on a field approximately 60 x 40-yards in dimension. Players are encouraged to use step-over move throughout the game situation. Players are also provided with information on depth, width, penetration and support as key concepts of the game.

Progression(s)

Allowing a wider field encourages more 1 v 1 situations to occur.

Diagram 11

40 yards

60 yards

Rangers F.C. Academy

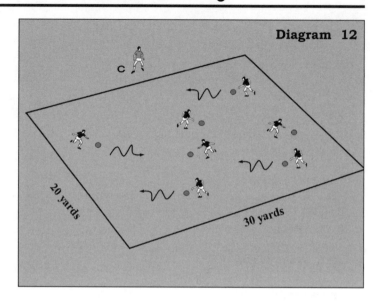

Diagram 12

Cool Down

In a defined 30 x 20-yard area with one ball, each player dribbles freely. Introduce a few basic static stretches to provide an understanding of the correct technique. Players are given homework each week to work on in advance of the next session.

These sessions take place at the state-of-the-art Rangers Football Training Center, Murray Park, where the first team players train on a daily basis. Murray Park is recognized as one of the most modern and state of the art facilities in European football boasting six top quality grass pitches, an outdoor floodlit new generation Astroturf pitch, fitness training area, hydrotherapy pool, and indoor new generation training pitch.

Training Overlaps

The following series of drills focusing on overlaps are presented by Wayne Harrison, Director of Player and Coach Development for Eden Prairie Soccer Club in Minnesota. Harrison is also the author of a number of best-selling coaching books. This is part two of a two-part series. Part One appeared in the January/February issue.

Progression(s)

Here (4) works the overlap with (2) from the back into midfield.

Focus on the mechanics of the overlap itself and do not worry that (3) is left with a 2 v 1 if his team loses the ball, that's another topic. We want to set the condition to make sure all over the field overlaps are being practiced in the game situation.

Develop: Introduce the idea of (2) using overlapping player (4) as a decoy. For example, if the defender moves over to cover (4's) run then it means (6) is free for (2) to pass the ball to.

Alternately, if (6) moves away to create space for (2) to move into, then (2) can bring the ball inside and keep possession of it until the right pass presents itself.

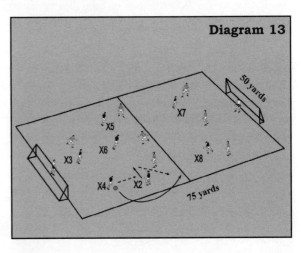

Diagram 13

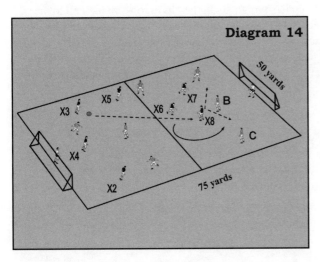

Diagram 14

Progression(s)

Continuing on with the theme, if a long pass is played forward and the run to overlap is too far for the passer for it to be realistic, then the next closest player must perform the overlap.

Here (3) plays a good ball forward into the feet of (8) who comes short to receive. (6) effects an overlap run around (8) and I have shown two possible eventualities. (8) can pass to overlapping player (6) or if, for example, (B) is drawn to (8) coming inside with the ball and (C) covers the overlapping run of (6) then (8) can pass to (7) who is in a free position to shoot at goal.

The situations created by a simple overlap run are endless. The point is that such a run unsettles defenses and players should be encouraged to make them. They must be aware also that they are making the run not just for themselves, but also unselfishly for a team mate to receive the pass instead.

Working both ways, this is a quick transition play session using wide players as the focal points to ensure we get lots of overlap plays and crosses in. You can overload areas where you want, for instance, if your players are particularly poor in finishing, have only one defender against two attackers and so on. You can determine any strategy you like and tailor the session to the number of players you have to work with. Players have to overlap the wide player when they pass the ball to them and get the cross in unopposed. Wide players perform in channels and no defenders can encroach into these zones, ensuring a constant supply of crosses both ways. They stay in the attacking half of the field. The field is short and tight to make sure lots of crossing and finishing takes place at both ends of the field.

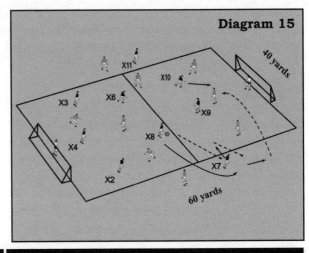

Diagram 15

Training Overlaps

Progression(s)

Here player (2) has passed the ball long to player (11) so we are looking at the closest player making the overlap run to receive the pass and get the cross into the penalty area. (6) performs this run. If the defender is close enough to work the overlap with the wide midfielder, then they can do that also. We need to encourage defenders to join in the attack whenever and where ever possible.

(F) can't track the run of (6), so (6) can make an effective overlap run and get a cross in. Both teams get the chance here to effect overlap runs. You can condition it where (11) stays inside and (6) stays outside until the next transition, or switch back as soon as the overlap play is completed.

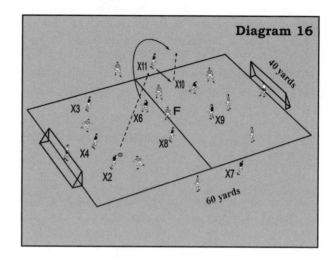

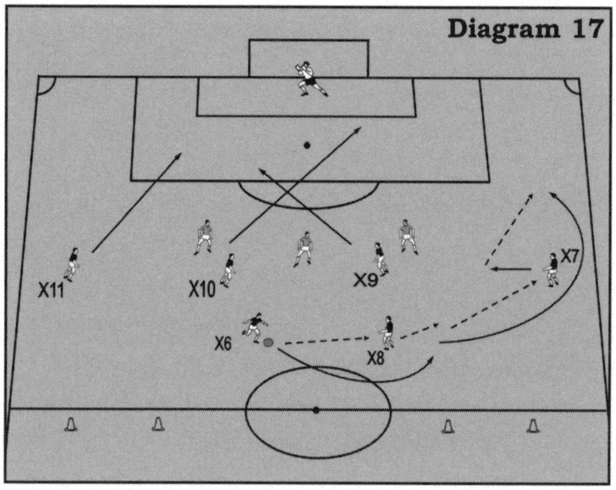

Diagram 16

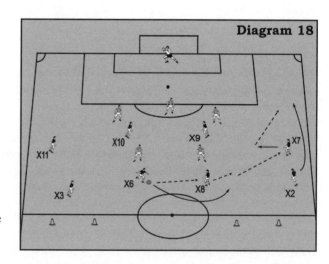

Diagram 17

An overlap play to begin the move with (8) and (6). (6) then passes to (7) and makes an overlap run to receive the pass and get into the crossing position.

If the defenders win the ball, they have to work the ball to the target goals and the play begins again. The end product for the attacking team is an overlap, a cross and a finish on goal. As we have no wide defenders the overlap movement will be effected every time, so players get success; gain confidence and experience while making it work. Work both sides of the field.

To make it competitive, every time the defenders win it and get it to the target, it is a goal to them. Every time the attacking team get a finish on target, it is a goal to them (or they have to score).

Progression(s)

Still in an overload situation to help gain success and breed confidence in the players, introduce two fullbacks into the game and some more defenders, building up the numbers in the session.

Primarily working with the wide players and how they create positions to cross the ball from. For your preparation, you can play against a back-four or a back-three depending on what the opposition play like (better to plan for both!!).

Coaching Points
- Does the player need support behind or in front?
- Create Space – move inside with the ball to open it up outside
- Communication – support player can call "Hold" to gain time to get into position
- Timing of the run – go wide (angle and distance)
- Player on the ball passes or uses the run as a decoy to come inside and attack

Diagram 18

Training Overlaps

Progression(s)

You can set it up where (6) passes the ball in or a fullback begins the play. Both will happen in the actual game.

We have gone from no opposition in wide areas so we are guaranteed an overlap and cross, to a 2 v 1 in our favor in a wide area of the field. We should still be good for making an overlap run effective.

If (F) stood in the passing lane getting the ball to (2) on the overlap, the move could be completed by (7) passing inside to (9) who can play a 1 or 2 touch passing movement into the path of (2's) run.

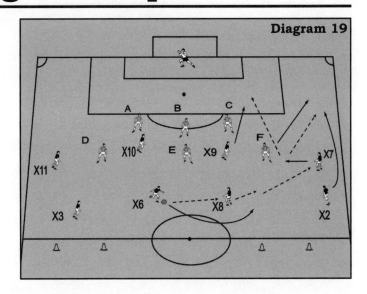

Diagram 19

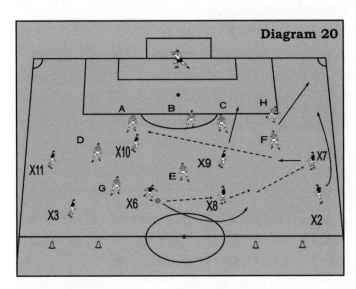

Diagram 20

Building the session up so it is more game related, we bring in more players on the defending team. The attacking team have to really work to be effective in wide areas, making overlapping runs and getting crosses in.

It is more a 2 v 2 situation now. Introduce the concept of the decoy now. Here defender (H) has tracked the run of (2) and stopped the pass so (7) needs to consider other options (see above). Now (7) passes the ball inside because (2) has taken (H) away from the space inside. (7) may attack the goal and get a shot in from this position also. There are various movements that can happen here.

This is effected by the overlap run of (2) joining in the attack in a wide area.

An example of an overlapping situation in an 11 v 11 game. This is the most likely area the overlap will occur, in the wide areas of the field.

It should effect an overload with a 2 v 1 advantage to the attacking team in this set up of the teams. If it is a man marking back four, then (B) will be uncomfortable to leave (9) and this should allow (2) time and space to make the cross into the box.

If (B) closes down (2), then this may free up (9) who will be in position to receive a pass from (2) as (B) is closing and is perhaps caught in no man's land. Whichever reaction occurs, the overlap is creating a healthier position for the attacking team.

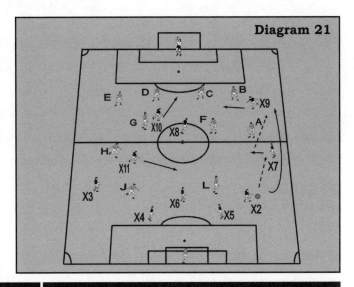

Diagram 21

Fulham F.C. Academy

These sessions are provided by Rob Gale of Score UK/Fulham Academy and are part of the coaching curriculum he has used at the Fulham Academy.

Passing & Receiving

The players face each other three feet apart. One ball for each pair, passing back and forth. Players work as fast as they can and count the passes.

Coaching Points

- Use Inside of foot - lock ankle square to target
- Up on toes to receive pass - move into line with the ball
- Communication - must call partners name

Progression

- Set time limit or limit to one touch
- Use weaker foot only
- Players must control with one foot and pass with the other

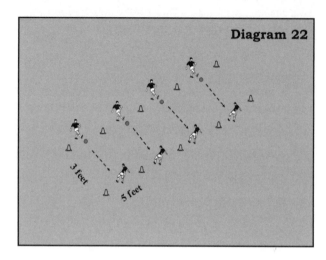

Diagram 22

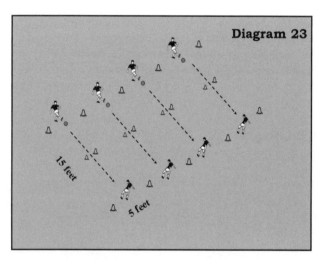

Diagram 23

Passing & Receiving

The set up is similar as before but the players are now 15 feet away from each other with two cones two feet apart in the middle. Pass back and forth with each pass, passing through the cones.

Coaching Points

- Try to be quick, but maintaining accuracy
- Up on toes to receive pass - move into line with the ball
- Help partner with straight passes

Progression

- Condition passing foot
- Reduce time / increase distance
- Players must control with one foot and pass with the other
- If players miss passing through cones, score returns to zero

Passing & Receiving

Same set up as before. The first player passes through the cones. The receiver controls ball with outside of right foot and plays ball back down side of cones to his partner. Pass back and forth using both feet. Reverse roles.

Coaching Points

- Players use inside of foot to control and take across body
- Use disguise before making move and playing ball back to partner
- Place time limit on players count passes

Progression

- Use markers as defenders
- Take ball out of feet and make crisp pass
- Look up before passing
- Quick change of feet to make faster return pass

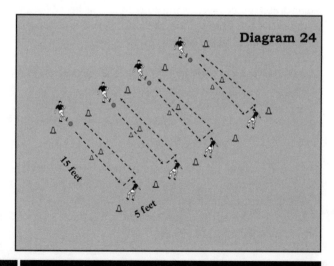

Diagram 24

Fulham F.C. Academy

Passing & Receiving

In groups of fours - X1 and X2 face each other and X3 and X4 face each other. X1 and X4 have soccer balls. X1 and X4 pass to middle where X2 and X3 return pass and spin to face other end players. Repeat.

Coaching Points
- Accuracy to maintain speed of drill
- Communicate when you want to pass
- Central players use each other as defenders to spin off
- Up on toes - lock ankle square especially on volleys

Progression
- Rotate positions
- Limit time
- Condition playing foot
- Throw balls in and get volleys back

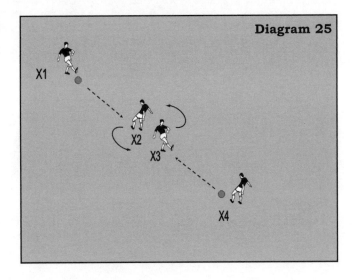

Diagram 25

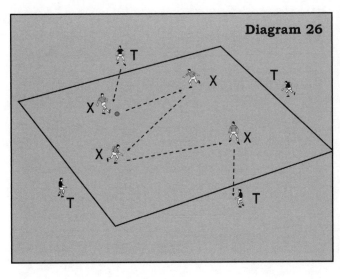

Diagram 26

Passing & Movement

In a 12 x 15-yard grid, four X players on inside and four T players on outside. T plays ball into any X who play one-touch passing. After four passes, X plays back to any T who repeats with a pass into X.

Coaching Points
- Quality of pass - accuracy and weight
- Support and body positions
- Movement of players - angle and distance
- Communication of all players

Progression
- Condition passing feet
- Make T control pass with one touch

Passing & Movement

X1 passes to X2 who takes two touches. X2 plays into X3 who sets up X1 to play to X4. Repeat from opposite side starting with X4.

Coaching Points
- Quality of pass - accuracy and weight
- Create space - long/short - open up for passes
- Timing and angle of movement from middle players

Progression
- Condition passing feet and number of touches
- Introduce lofted passes for longer passes
- Increase space and distance if necessary

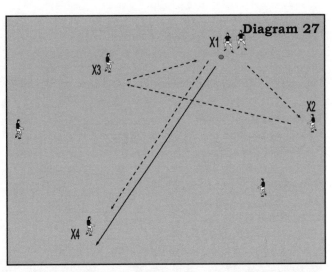

Diagram 27

Fulham F.C. Academy

Passing & Movement

X1 passes to X2 who takes two touches. X2 plays into X3 who sets up for X4 to play to X on end line. Repeat from opposite side with X starting and X3 and X4 reversing roles.

Coaching Points

- Quality of pass - accuracy and weight
- Create space - long/short - open up for passes
- Timing and angle of movement from middle players

Progression

- Condition passing feet and number of touches
- Introduce lofted passes for longer passes
- Increase space and distance if necessary

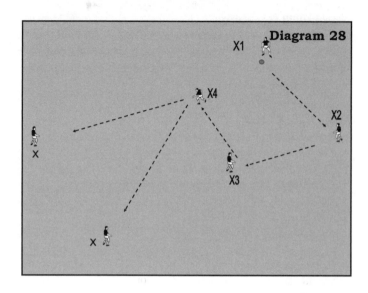

Passing & Movement

X1 passes to X2 who takes two touches. X2 plays into X4 who sets back for X1. X4 spins off left shoulder. X1 passes to X3 who lays off to X4 to play forward.

Coaching Points

- Same as previous drill
- Timing and direction of X4's spin
- Concentrate of quality of set up - angles of support and communication are vital

Progression

- Repeat from both ends

Passing & Movement

X1 passes to X2 who take two touches. X2 plays into X4 who sets back for X1. X4 spins off right shoulder. X1 plays ball down line for X3 who has run into space vacated by X4. X3 plays forward or switches to X4.

Coaching Points

- Quality of passes and set up - accuracy and weight
- Create space
- Support position of X3
- Movement of X4 - sideways on

Progression

- Repeat from both ends
- Rotate all players in each of these drills

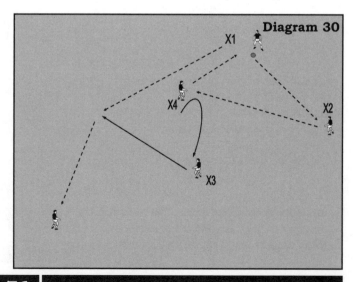

Manchester United Soccer Schools

This session is submitted by Mike Neary, Residential Manager at Manchester United Soccer Schools. The aim and objective of the session is to develop a positive attitude to shooting for the whole squad. This will be done through technical and skill coaching and re-enforced during small-sided games, plus technical coaching where necessary. The MUSS philosophy is geared towards creating a positive, fun learning environment aiming to help players reach their optimum level of performance and instilling a lifelong passion for the game. MUSS understands the importance of developing young players' personal attributes as well as their technical and tactical ability.

Dynamic Flex Warm-Up
Players line up in groups of six and perform a 20-minute workout where flexibility in action is used to increase:
- Body temperature
- Heart rate, blood flow and breathing rate
- Elasticity of muscular system
- Mental alertness
- Activate the neuromuscular system

Coaching Points
- Where necessary all dr
  on the balls of the feet
- Exercises performed w
  movement
- Maintain correct arm mechanics
- Maintain an upright posture with head up
- Small and simple movements

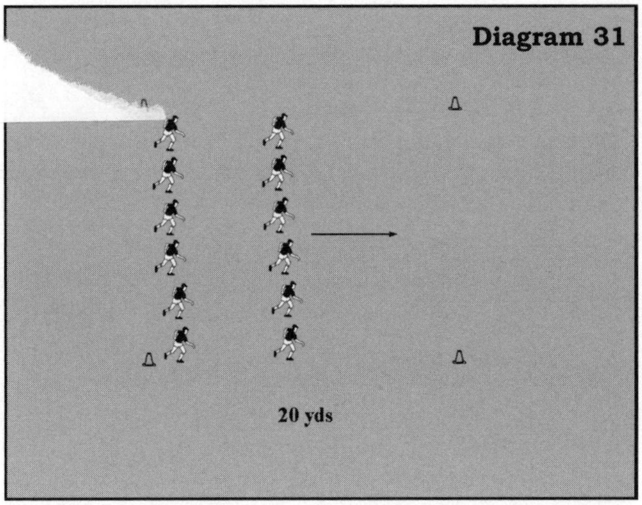

Example of Movements
- High knee across the body
- Hamstring flicks
- Heel toe
- High knee skip
- Russian walk
- Knee hug

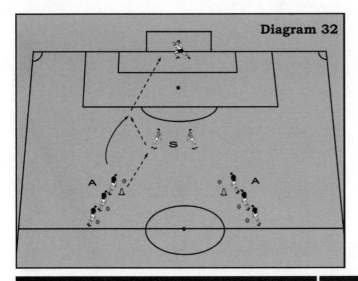

Diagram 31

20 yds

Shooting
Attacker (A) passes into server (S) and immediately overlaps S for the return pass. Once player A shoots, they retrieve the ball and join the opposite line to shoot with other foot.

Diagram 32

Coaching Points
- Awareness – check the GK position and aim for the far corner
- Relax – compose yourself and use your arms to stay balanced
- Head down - focus on the ball at the moment of contact
- To drive it low, place the non-kicking foot alongside the ball and strike through the mid-line of the ball
- For power – follow through with the kicking foot after the ball has been struck

Progression(s)
- Rotate server
- Vary the angle of the serve, left right, in front

Shooting (Continued)

Same set up as previous exercise. As soon as Attacker (A) passes to Server (S), Defender (D) can leave the starting position and close down (A) to put under pressure before they try and score.

Coaching Points
- Decision – when & where to shoot
- Technique – balanced, accurate, power
- Reaction – other players - alert but composed
- Attitude – precise and patient

Observations
- Attacker (A) controls the ball as quickly as possible playing it into their path before striking at goal
- Primarily, the attackers should get the shots on target, and increased power in the shot, will help it beat the goalkeeper

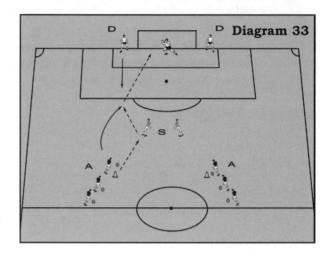

Shooting From Distance

Mark a 36 x 40-yard area with a halfway line 18 yards across the field and full-size goals. Both teams play 4 v 1 in shooting zone with shots only being made from behind the half-line. The front players set up shots for other players and follows in for rebounds.

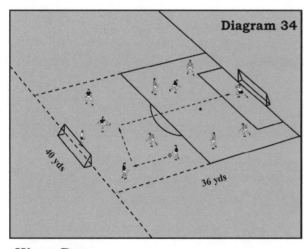

Coaching Points
- Create space/movement
- First touch
- Awareness
- Positive attitude - shoot if you can
- Technique - type of shot
- Power
- Shoot across the keeper
- Strikers to follow-in
- Be aware of alternatives if shot isn't on. Square pass, go back and keep possession

Progression
Play two-touch for all players.

Warm Down
- Begin with moderate dynamic flex movements
- Gradually reduce intensity
- Incorporate static stretching exercises of all major leg muscles

Dynamic Flex Cool Down
- Gastrocnemius stretch
- Abductors stretch
- Adductors stretch
- Hamstring stretch
- Quadriceps stretch
- Standing hurdles
- Standing high kicks
- High knee skips

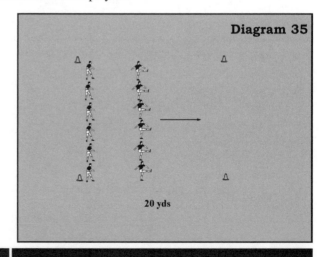

Sheffield United U15's

These agility and defending sessions are contributed by Sheffield United U15 coach, Sam Saif. Saif holds a EUFA "A" License and has over 15 years experience coaching at youth academies for professional clubs in England.

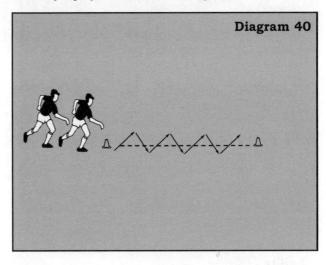

Diagram 40

Agility & Quickness
Players work across a 10-yard line.

Coaching Points
- Weight distribution
- Semi-crouched position
- Balance and coordination
- Quickness of feet movement

Progression(s)
- Players work along a 10-yard line

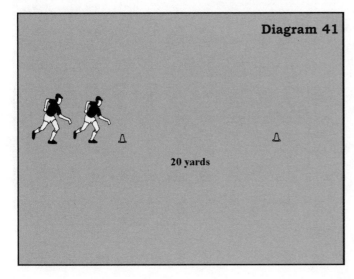

Diagram 41

20 yards

Agility & Quickness Double Touch Footwork
Players run through two cones, 20 yards apart.

Coaching Points
- Quickness of feet movement onto and off the ground
- Use of arms for balance and assisting technique
- Coordination and speed of lower and upper body movement

Progression(s)
- Forward movement
- Backward movement
- Open-hip movements
- Closed-hip movements
- Side step movement
- Side cross-step movement

Agility & Quickness Speed work
Players run various distances from 5 - 20 yards.

Coaching Points
- Fast foot pick up - linear running - high knee
- Use of arms for balance and technique
- Irregular foot patterns
- Change of direction
- Side step running

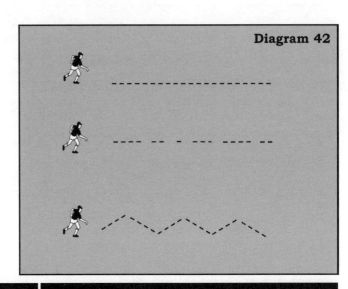

Diagram 42

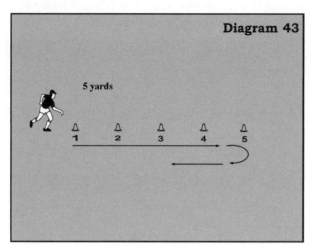

Diagram 43

5 yards

1 2 3 4 5

Agility

Five cones are placed five yards apart. Players line up at the first cone and sprint to close down on cone 5. Here they stop, then change direction under control and balance. They then back up to cone 3 in a jockeying posture, then turn and sprint inside or outside back to starting position.

Coaching Points
- Speed in closing down
- Technique in stopping
- Defending stance
- "Showing" in one direction
- Backward defending movement
  - show left
  - show right
  - square body position

Agility - (Fig 1)

Four cones are placed in a straight line five yards apart. X1 starts at cone one and closes down X2 who is at cone four. X2 runs outside cones, changing speed and direction and sprints to cone one. X1 shadows the movements of X2 and reacts to the sprint of X2. Work right side and left side.

Agility Clock - (Fig 2)

Five cones are set up with one center cone and others at right angles four yards away. Players start at the center cone upon coaches whistle, run to touch each cone, returning to the center cone each time.

Progression(s)
- Work right and left
- Turn right each time, then left each time

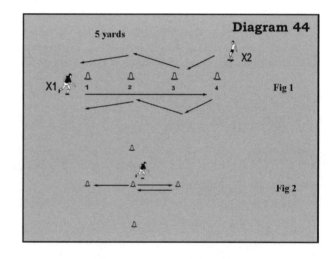

Diagram 44

5 yards

X2

X1   1   2   3   4   Fig 1

Fig 2

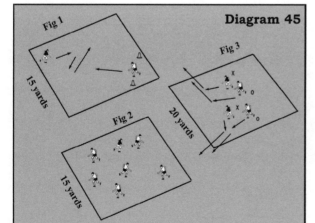

Diagram 45

Fig 1

15 yards

Fig 2

15 yards

Fig 3

20 yards

Agility Games
"Five Second Catch" - (Fig 1)

Players are inside a 15 yard grid. White player has five seconds to touch dark player who must run between cones.

"Six Man Catch" - (Fig 2)

Dark player must touch as many white's as possible in 20 seconds. Players have to stay inside the 10-yard grid at all times.

"Stay Tight" - (Fig 3)

In a 20-yard grid, X is touch-tight marked by O. With just one change of direction allowed, X must sprint outside the square. X jogs until ready to sprint. O must stay touch-tight close to X.

Triangle Work - (Fig 1)

Three cones are positioned to form a triangle. X starts at cone one and works around the triangle until back to cone one, then repeat in opposite direction immediately.

"V" Work - (Fig 2)

X starts at cone one and works four yards out and back to cones two and three alternately.

Coaching Points

- Speed of footwork in defending stance
- Turns in defending stance
- Changes of direction in the defending stance

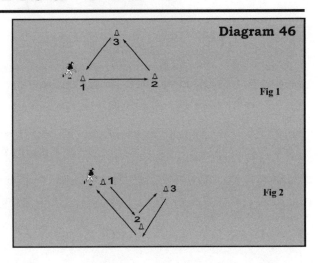

Diagram 46

Fig 1

Fig 2

Closing Down

Reading the situation
- The player in possession
- Your immediate opponent
- Other attacking and defensive players activity

Preparation to close down
- Focus of attention - ball, opponent
- Stance, movement, readiness

Timing of closing down
- When the pass is certain
- As it is released

The approach
- Speed
- Intention
- Angle
- Observation of the receiving player's activity
- Caution
- Controlled deceleration

Jockeying

Defenders intention and opponents characteristics

Playing situation on arrival

Limiting the opponents operating choices and options

Gaining control of the situation - distances, angles, changes of position

Possible and speedy changes of position and balance

Making play predictable

Patience and decision making
- Push opponents in which direction? Why?
- To "work" the opponent? To tackle?

Pressing - Jockeying

In a 15 x 15-yard grid, players line up in opposite diagonal corners. X2 serves ball to O1. X1 "presses" the ball as it travels to O1. O1 in possession attempts to dribble with the ball and carry it across the line between the two cones. X1 defends accordingly to stop O1 from achieving objective.

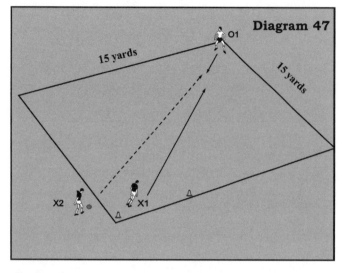

Diagram 47

Coaching Points
- When to close down
- How to close down
    - Speed
    - Angle
    - Awareness of possibilities for O1
- Pressing/Jockeying
    - Angle
    - Distance
    - Stance
    - Focus of attention
    - Feet movement
    - Turning
    - Working the opponent
    - Tackling

Jockeying

In a 15 x 30-yard grid, S serves ball into O1 to receive and turn. X1 closes down and defends against O1. O1 may use T on sideline for wall pass if needed. X1 to protect goal A or B as directed by coach. O1 to dribble through either goal to score.

Coaching Points
- Jockeying opponents
    - Speed of approach
    - Angle of approach
    - Distance of pressure
    - Stance
    - Focus of attention
    - Feet movement
    - Defending against a wall pass

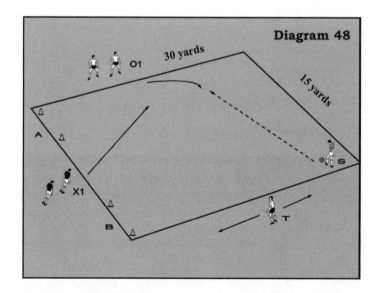

Diagram 48

Marking

To allow an opponent to receive a pass

To allow an opponent to receive a pass under limited and controllable conditions

To prevent an opponent from receiving a pass

To prevent an opponent from turning with the ball

To discourage the passer from releasing the ball to your opponents

"Skin-tight" marking

Marking and "tracking" another opponent

Prioritizing
Involves
• Distance
• Angle
• Stance, movement and changes of position
• Body position

Decisions
• Intercept and create
• Spoil and recover
• Contain and "stick"
• Tackle

Golden Goal

This goal was scored by Kevin Keegan in an FA Cup tie for Liverpool against West Ham United in 1976. This is a classic goal that highlights the benefits of two central strikers working together. During this time, Keegan was partnered with John Toshack up front for Liverpool and their partnership was one of the most feared of their day.

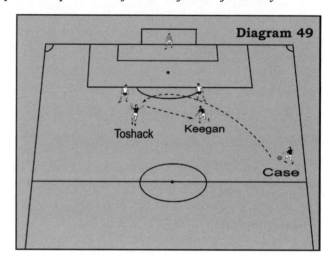

Jimmy Case crosses the ball in from just inside the attacking half. Toshack is just outside the penalty area and heads the ball to Keegan's feet.

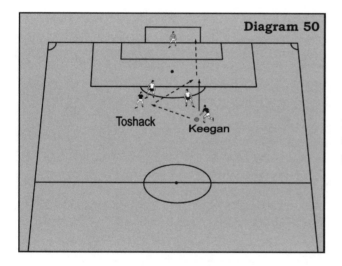

Keegan controls the ball, plays a give-and-go with Toshack and then volley's the ball to the near post for a memorable goal.

David Platt

WORLD CLASS COACHING is pleased to announce a relationship with David Platt for the former England National Team captain and England U21 coach to write a "Tactical" article in this and each of the next five issues. Platt is now the head of Advanced Football Knowledge, a company that provides training courses for soccer coaches directly through the internet at www.afkuk.co.uk. This article discusses the merits of playing with three or four defenders.

The most suitable formation to play is a question that all coaches are constantly trying to answer. The shift from a traditional 4-4-2 was made as coaches looked to get an extra central midfielder, opting to move a defender forward, going to three at the back and effectively playing with a 3-5-2. To counter act this, the 4-3-3 evolved, ensuring the extra midfielder and also giving tactical problems to the 3-5-2 as with three forwards to now mark the three defenders had problems and needed help from other quarters. While possible to do, it is far easier to deal with three forwards with a flat back four than it is with only three defenders, which has led to most teams now operating in 4-4-2 or 4-3-3 formations. In the European Championships of 2004 held in Portugal, 15 of the 16 countries involved played with four at the back. Only the eventual winners Greece operated with a "three", and even then, when they faced teams playing with a 4-3-3 they themselves reverted to a back four to retain a spare man.

Playing with a flat back four makes it much easier for the defenders to stay in contact with each other and minimize the spaces that can be exploited by the opposition. It is easier to coach and make everyone aware of their jobs than it is when operating with a three at the back because other players have to be made aware of when and how to help defend. Also, the movements made by the defense when closing down are more dramatic, which leads to a lack of synchronisation and distances between them grow to where they can be exploited.

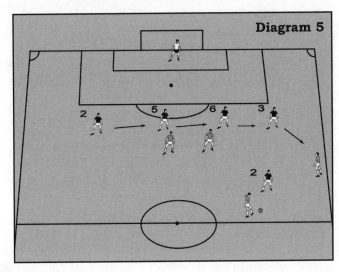

In this diagram, we show a flat back four dealing with the opposition coming down the right hand side of the pitch. As stated above, the movements of the back four are shorter and easier to do in unison than we see in the next diagram with the same situation, but operating with a back three. The movement made by the defenders in the next diagram can be negated if the wing back is asked to defend deeper, but the consequence of this is that a central midfielder would have to be the player closing down the fullback advancing with the ball.

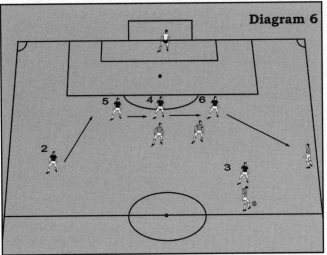

In my opinion, defending with a flat back four is far more resolute when it comes to negating the opposition's chances of scoring than when defending with a "three". However, if a team wishes to play out from the back and set up its attacks, this opinion is reversed. Although a back four can spread out across the pitch and receive the ball from the goalkeeper to begin to start attacks, two opposition forwards can negate this a lot easier than they can do when faced with a back three spread across the pitch. The angles that three players spread out across the pitch create are much better than they are when four players do the same. Furthermore, there are more players already in more prominent attacking positions.

David Platt

In this diagram, we see the angles created by a flat back four and how two forwards can negate this, while in the next diagram, the same situation is replicated, but with a back three. The problem with a back four is that there is no central player as such. Therefore, in order to get out from the back, it has to be a fullback who does so and he can be closed down with a simple sideways movement by one of the strikers with his partner shuffling across to help. An effective switch has to be made to get out the other side, but again all the forwards have to do is shuffle across as the ball is traveling. However, with a back three, due to a player being central, he can be the fulcrum to start the attack and instead of having only two players (fullbacks) who can get out with the ball, all three can do so.

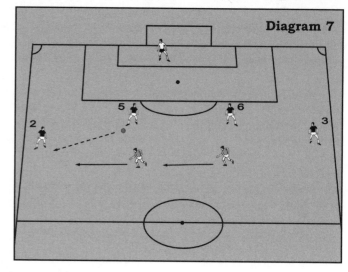

Diagram 7

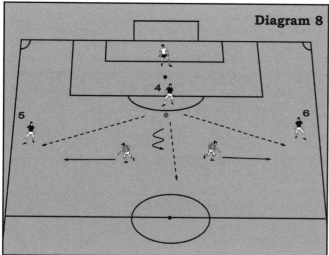

Diagram 8

If all this is true, then a coach needs to make a decision that is best for his team. Do I defend better and more resolutely by operating with a flat back four or do I play with three at the back and make it easier to start attacks?

This however, would be a closed mind and the modern day coach has to be creative to progress. Many years ago there was a fluidity about formations which then gave way to tactical discipline and shape, but the improved physical capabilities of players have now turned this back whereby fluid formations are now much more apparent than they were around 20 years ago.

In the World Cup of 2002 held in Japan / Korea, Brazil won the tournament playing very offensive soccer, but still conceding few goals.

Luis Felipe Scolari had players that were all comfortable on the ball and recognized that in one player (Edmilson) had the key to being able to defend as a flat back four but start attacks as a back three without it being static and stage managed.

David Platt

Here we see how the Brazilians spread out into their attacking shape when the goalkeeper has the ball. Cafu and Roberto Carlos, (2 & 3), two very offensive minded fullbacks, pushed right up to the half way line with the two center halves, Roque Junior & Lucio (6 & 4), spreading across the pitch. The other players started in positions similar to what is shown. If they could play out from the back like this, then they would do so, however if needed, Edmilson (5), would drop in to a defensive fulcrum position, and the other players would react accordingly to make a back three more akin to what we showed earlier. Any of these three would then be free to go forward with the ball and leave the other two players to mark and cover, content to go 2 v 2 with the forwards.

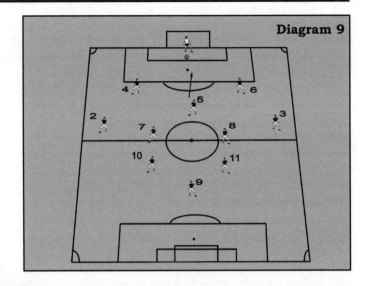

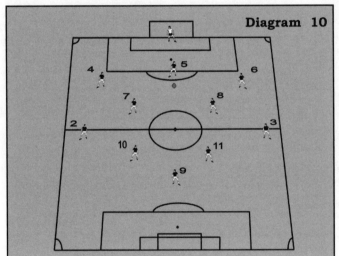

These tactics of Brazil meant they could play in a very offensive manner and that no matter who they came up against, they could always stay loyal to their philosophy of playing football on the ground, keeping possession and being attractive and very offensive in their outlook.

While simple in its design, this tactic does need good players with the right characteristics. However, Brazil had these and were willing to attempt to do it at the highest level. As development for young players it is also a good way of playing as it encourages tactical intelligence and a type of soccer which I am sure we all want to play.

England National Team

This article was written by Dave Clarke, Head Women's Coach at Quinnipiac University in Connecticut. The notes were provided by Martin Tierney of www.Soccerexperience.com. England National Team Training Session - June 1, 2001 La Manga, Spain, six days before a World Cup qualifier against Greece in Athens.

Assistant coaches Sammy Lee and Peter Taylor are at the field early to prepare all the equipment needed for when the players arrive. The keepers are with them and they do some stretching and exercises off to the side before the other players arrive. The field players arrive with head coach Sven Goran Eriksson about 30 minutes later. All the players are dressed the same, wearing England training gear and the coaches are all dressed in the same coaching gear with their socks pulled up as usual.

Warm-Up

The team splits into two groups, one with bibs and one with no bibs. The players jog anywhere on the field without a ball, occasionally stopping for individual stretching.

After 6-7 minutes they come back into the coaches, but only Sammy Lee speaks to the players. The players continue the warm-up in pairs, working on various types of ball control with the service out of the hand. After stopping for a group stretch, they continue to work with the same partner while passing and moving all over the field.

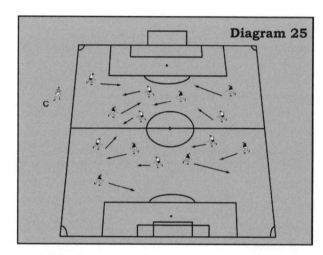

Warm-Up Game

The two teams split into a game of handball with two full size goals on a field 25 yards long.

Emphasis: no standing around and goals only scored with a header or volley.

The main training session is then split into two with a group each for Taylor and Lee. They both do the same activities.

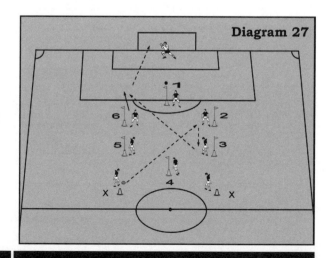

Activity One

X plays passes to player 2. Player 2 lays the ball back to player 3. Player 3 passes in front of player 6 who then shoots on his first or second touch. Players rotate positions and the next ball is played from the other line.

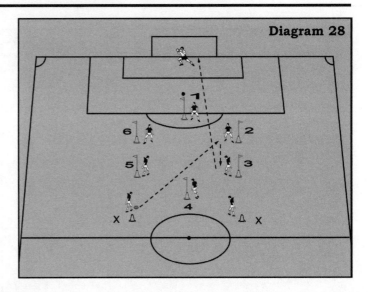

Diagram 28

Activity Two

X plays the ball to player 2. Player 2 lays the ball back for player 3 or player 5 who shoot on first or second touch. This was much easier and caused less confusion. It was one pass and then one lay off, followed by a finish. The players continue to rotate positions and the ball now starts from the opposite line.

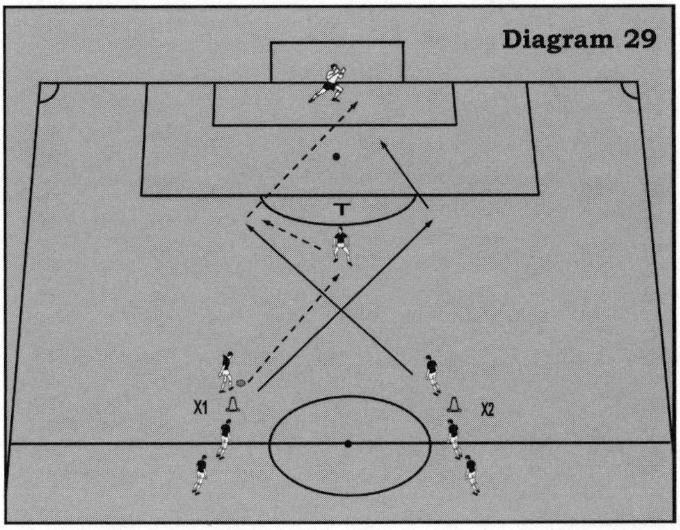

Diagram 29

Activity Three

The ball is played from one of the lines to the center forward/target player who controls the ball - the two players at the front of each line make a crossover run. The center forward turns and lays off to one of the two players to finish. The other follows in for any rebound. The players rotate lines and the forward is changed every minute.

Emphasis: good pass with pace into the forward, good runs off the ball, good control and lay off, quality finishing with everything done at speed.

Activity Four

One of the two players at the start of the lines takes the ball and heads for goal. He fakes to shoot, but then stops the ball or back heels it for the player from the other line to follow and finish. The next ball starts with the player from the opposite line.

Emphasis: direct run from the player with the ball, good communication, good lay off and good timing of the lay off followed by a quality finish. This was a very simple activity that the players really enjoyed and seemed to get more out of than the first two.

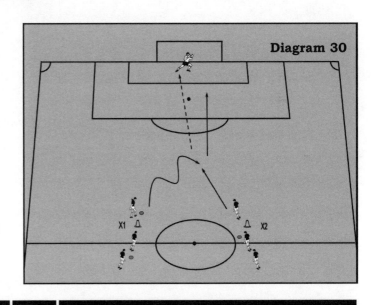

Diagram 30

England National Team

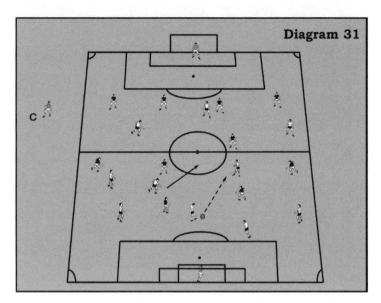

Diagram 31

Game

Sammy Lee then takes the players for a group stretching and exercise session for about 10-15 minutes.

The players are then split up into two teams with a first 11 and a second 11.

The game is played at a fairly high pace, but far from a 100% level.

At the end of the game the teams come together for stretching and cool down session, conducted again by Sammy Lee.

Observations

The full session from start to finish lasted just over 90 minutes.

The English coaching staff was very professional; everything was planned and organized in every detail. The balls were pumped, bibs laid out and the field was marked out with cones and flags before the players even arrived.

Eriksson said very little to his team in a coaching context throughout the session, which was very strange to observe. All he did was watch the session and talk to his assistants.

Everything was at no more than 75% effort, which is to be understood considering all these players had just finished 60 to 70 games for their club teams.

The speed of play was excellent and the quality of passing and moving was of the highest order.

The level of communication between the players was very high and the players were constantly talking and looking for the ball.

Footnote:

England played Greece in a World Cup qualifier at the Olympic Stadium in Athens on June 6, 2001. They won 2-0 with goals from Paul Scholes (64) and David Beckham (87) and the win ultimately helped them to qualify for the 2002 World Cup in Japan and Korea.

The starting line was: Seaman, Neville P, Ashley Cole, Gerrard, Keown, Ferdinand, Beckham, Scholes (Butt 88), Fowler (Smith 79), Owen, Heskey (McManaman 74).

Sheffield United U15's

This is part two of a defending session by Sheffield United U15 coach, Sam Saif. Part One appeared in the March/April issue. Saif holds a EUFA "A" License and has over 15 years experience coaching at youth academies for professional clubs in England.

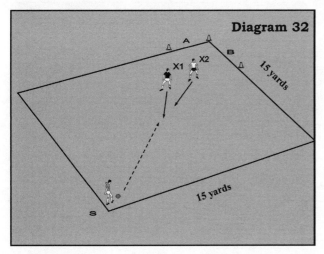

Diagram 32

Defending

In a 15 x 15-yard grid, S serves to X1 who is marked from behind by X2. X1 should attempt to turn and beat X2 to run with the ball between gate A or gate B as directed by the coach. X2 should defend against X1 and protect the gate directed by the coach.

Coaching Points
- Marking
- Preventing opponents from turning
  - Distance from opponent
  - Stance
  - Focus of attention
  - Feet movement
  - Challenging for the ball

Defending

Field area of 25 x 25-yards in and around the penalty area. Pairs are numbered 1 to 4. The coach calls a number and that pair (one a nominated attacker, the other a defender) come to a ball passed by the coach. Attacker attempts to score, while the defender prevents the attack.

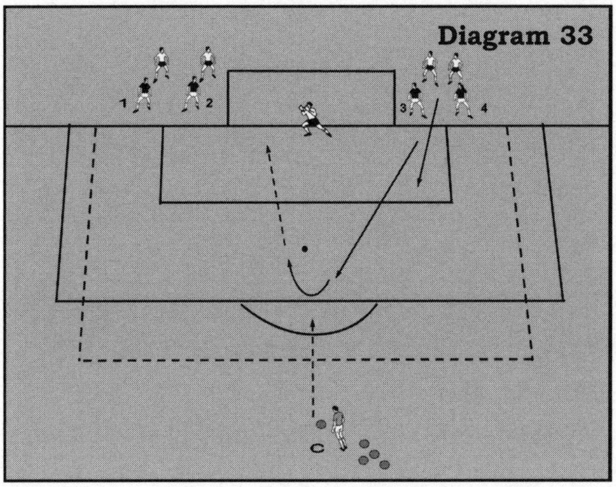

Coaching Points
- Marking
- "Approaching" the ball
- Preventing opponents from turning
  - Distance from opponent
  - Stance
  - Focus of attention
  - Feet movement
  - Challenging for the ball
- If two pairs are called
  - Press and cover
  - Defend against wall pass, take overs and overlaps
  - Shot blocking
  - Rebounding

Diagram 33

Pressing

Moving into a position within 2-3 yards of an opponent.

Reducing passing angles and space in which to operate for the player in possession.

Making passing targets predictable.

Forcing technical and tactical errors by making opponents perform quicker than they are capable of.

Through combined actions, forcing opponents to employ skills often outside their technical range, resulting in the team regaining possession.

A group and team response to regain possession of the ball.

Team compactness.

Sheffield United U15's

Pressing

Two teams play 6 v 6 for 45 seconds using approximately one quarter of a regular field. One player rests and counts the interceptions and losses of possession as a result of the "pressing tactic". X's (the majority) play possession football. O's (the minority) press to destroy possession. Change teams and roles at the end of 45 seconds.

Coach starts each game by passing to team in majority. O's press as a team to destroy possession by forcing the ball out of playing area. Coach immediately releases another ball to the majority. At the end of 45 seconds, count the losses of possession.

Coaching Points
- Who? presses the ball
- How? with what intention
- When? does the press begin
- Reaction/responsibilities of others
- Prevent the change of play

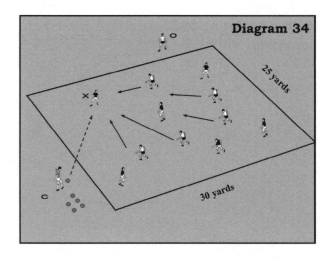

Diagram 34

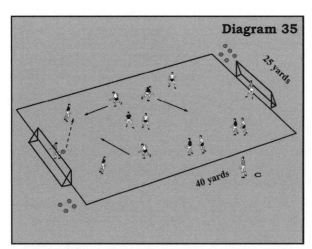

Diagram 35

Pressing

Two teams play 6 v 6 , 7 v 7, 8 v 8, etc. Have a supply of balls behind each goal. Coach calls a color, and the GK can distribute to any of those players.

Coaching Points
- Team "out" of possession works on pressing
- Who? presses the ball
- How? with what intention
- When? does the press begin
- Reaction/responsibilities of others
  - Mark
  - Track
  - Cover
  - Recover

Man Marking

Two teams play 7 v 7 on a 40 x 70-yard field. Five pairs of players who mark on man-for-man basis. One sweeper on each team with three-touch limit and can play in own half only.

Coaching Points
- Who to mark?
- How to mark?
- Tight and loose marking
- Defending in 1 v 1 situations
- Responsibilities "off the ball"
- Defending against "combination play"
- Defending when the ball is played beyond you, towards your goal
- Defending for beaten in 1 v 1

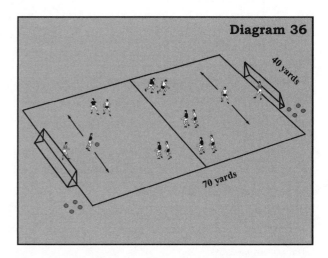

Diagram 36

Sheffield United U15's

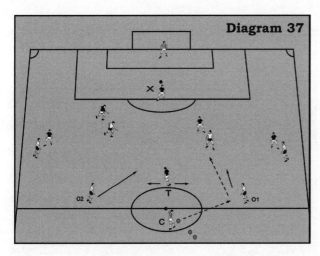

Diagram 37

Sweeper Role

Using half a field, attacking to one large goal, play six attackers against five defenders and a goalkeeper. Coach plays to O1 or O2 who feed and support other attackers, and have a maximum of three touches. O's play to score, X's play to gain possession and break over halfway line using "T" to assist.

Coaching Points

Markers
- As previous practice

Sweeper
- Positioning - behind, ahead of the defense
- Movement - according to the ball and attacking play
- Responsibilities:
    - When the ball is outside shooting distance
    - Inside shooting distance
    - At a strikers feet
    - Ball being "run" at the penalty box
    - Ball in wide position
    - On gaining possession

Defending With A Sweeper

Using a full sized regular field, teams play 11 v 11. Coach plays the ball to the goalkeeper, who passes out to a defender. Both teams play to score.

Coaching Points

- Role of sweeper and defenders
- Role of midfielders
- Role of strikers - according to the ball and attacking play
- Team compactness
- "Sliding" by midfielders and strikers across the field
- Defending responsibilities and team cohesion

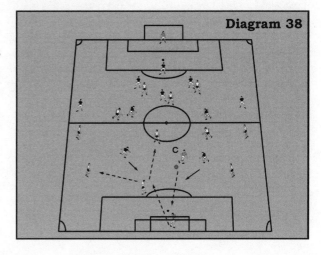

Diagram 38

Golden Goal

This goal was scored by a young Steve McManaman for Liverpool in a F.A. Cup quarter final game against Leeds United in 1986. This goal is a great example of how clinical, quick combination play around the penalty area can be.

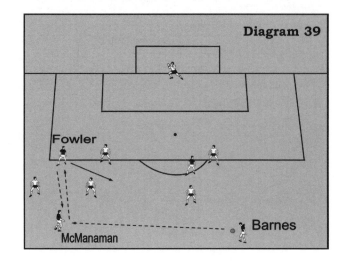

John Barnes plays the ball across the field to Steve McManaman who controls the ball and plays it forward to Robbie Fowler.

Fowler returns the pass to McManaman and then moves back and inside to receive the ball again.

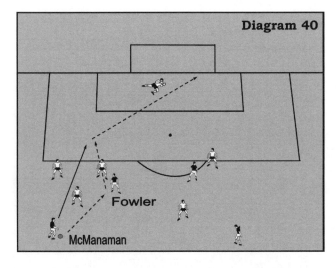

McManaman passes the ball back to Fowler who plays a give-and-go through the defender's legs for McManaman to run onto. McManaman places his shot neatly in the far corner.

Glasgow Rangers F.C.

Observed by Mike Saif. The session was conducted at the Murray Park, Rangers Academy. Murray Park is a state-of-the art facility with numerous outdoor fields (some with under soil heating), an artificial field, indoor field as well as the Rangers F.C. offices. Both the professional and youth teams train at Murray Park.

This shooting and finishing session was conducted by the coach of the U11 team, Craig Mullholland. The session was conducted indoors on Fieldturf due to heavy rain, making it impossible to train outdoors.

Warm-Up
In a 20 x 40-yard area, each player dribbles a ball around, practicing different fakes and moves. The coach then asks one player to demonstrate a move. All the players then practice that move. For the next few minutes, 4 - 5 players are asked to demonstrate a move for the other players to practice.

The players then go through a series of fast-feet exercises including pushing the ball side to side using the insides of the feet, pushing the ball forward using the sole of each foot, pulling the ball backwards using the sole of each foot, drag ball sideways with sole of each foot, etc. This is followed by some dynamic stretching and more fast-feet exercises. The total warm-up lasted about 25 minutes.

The players then have 25 minutes speed work with the Rangers Speed Coach, Charlie Affleck, before heading back to Craig Mullholland for the shooting and finishing part of the session.

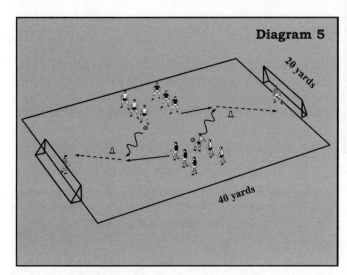

Diagram 5

Shooting and Finishing # 1
The white players dribble toward the cone, which is about 12 yards from goal. He then stops the ball for the dark player who times his run and then shoots. The players then join the back of the opposite line.

Both groups go at the same time. Play for 3 - 4 minutes and then start from the opposite side to shoot with the opposite foot.

Coaching Points
• Hit the target
• Pass the ball into the corner of the goal

Shooting and Finishing # 2
The lines of players are five yards apart. The white player passes to the dark player and then challenges him. The dark player opens up with one touch and then shoots.

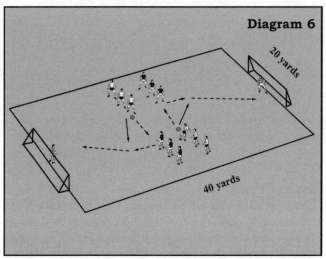

Diagram 6

Glasgow Rangers F.C.

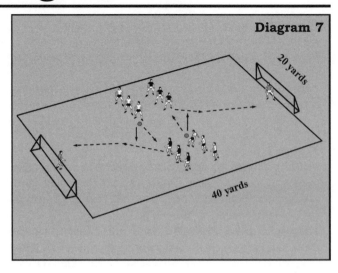

Diagram 7

Shooting and Finishing # 3

This is a progression from the previous exercise. This time the receiving player plays his first touch across the path of the challenging player, in an attempt to cut him off.

Diagram 8

Shooting and Finishing # 4

X1 passes to X 2 and then moves onto the field to play with X2. As soon as X2 receives the ball, the defender becomes active and challenges, creating a 2 v 1 situation with X1 and X2. The offside rule is in effect as X1 and X2 attempt to score.

After a shot or loss of possession, X1 moves to D, X2 moves behind X3 and D moves to X2. X3 passes to X4 to start the exercise again.

Coaching Points

- X2 looks to shoot or pass, depending on what the defender does

Shooting Game

Each team has four field players and two target players (one on either side of the goal they are attacking). A goal can be scored with or without using the target players.

Progression

The target players are moved to the field for a 7 v 7 scrimmage to end practice.

Coaching Points

The coach didn't stop either game much - when he did, it was almost always to focus on a shooting element.

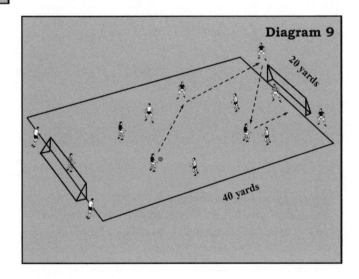

Diagram 9

Soccer Homework

Practice ended with a five-minute cool down and stretch. The coach then gave the players soccer homework to do before the next practice. At this point, he checked how the players were coming along with previously given homework. One of the players then demonstrated his juggling ability by juggling 25 times with his head and then each foot and thigh in turn.

David Platt

Contributed by David Platt, former England Captain and U21 coach - now head of www.afkuk.co.uk.

The modern day game requires the coach to have a knowledge and understanding of many aspects and be able to coach his players the different tactics required to win a match. While there are many different aspects that go into producing a performance, in simplistic terms you either have the ball and are therefore attacking, or the opposition have it and you are thus defending.

The top coaches in the world today focus on 5 issues surrounding the game which I have called the 5 Pillars. There are 2 pillars concerned with offensive play, 2 with defensive and then Set Pieces make the 5th. Offensive play is broken down into two categories, (1) In possession with the opposition unset and (2) In possession with the opposition set and similarly defensively (3) out of possession and team unset and (4) out of possession and team set.

In Possession With the Opposition Unset

This situation arises at the moment when the team wins the ball back from the opposition and lasts for circa 6 seconds against a well organized team. This time span is the optimum amount when a goal can be scored, taking advantage of the likely spread out nature of the opposition who have been in attacking mode. They are likely to have an offensive mind as a unit and will undoubtedly be searching to get back into a defensive shape, but the time it takes to do this leaves them vulnerable to the counter-attack, with defenders exposed individually and not being afforded any cover. This is an area the coach must spend time with his players on, devising strategies to take advantage of the turnover of the ball. To be successful in the game today, a team must defend in a manner to counter-attack, i.e.; stop the opposition from scoring at the same time as understanding that the ball will be lost and for a brief period on winning it there is the maximum opportunity to punish them. Many of the World's top teams have Transition players playing for them, players that take up half and half positions when defending, ready to fill holes and aid the defensive strategy if needed, but also in positions to be able to effect the counter-attack if the ball is won.

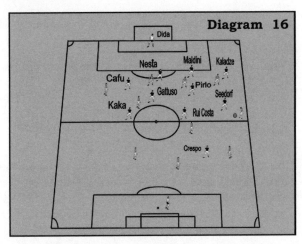

A.C. Milan are one of the best teams to do this, with Kaka & Shevchenko always in positions when the rest of the team is defending where they can help out if needed but can receive the ball when it is won. In the game today this phase is the most important one in open play and is statistically responsible for over 1/3rd of all goals scored. While it cannot be overestimated how important this phase is, it is equally important to recognize when the counter-attack possibility is over and possession of the ball is the correct phase.

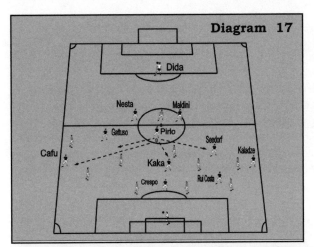

In Possession With the Opposition Set

This is an area which needs to be addressed, as a counter-attack opportunity can quickly fizzle out due to a foul, a misplaced pass or a well organized team which negates the counter-attack by keeping/getting many players behind the ball. It is important in this phase to circulate the ball, provide options backwards, forwards and square for the man on the ball and to create space through movement and rotation to try to open the defensive block up so that it can be exploited. Too much risk in this area can lead to being counter-attacked so covering your attacks must also be a focus when rehearsing your offensive moves.

Out Of Possession and the Team Unset

The importance of covering the attack cannot be stressed enough. Pushing too many players forward in search of a goal can be very risky as there is vulnerability about your shape, immediately you lose the ball. It is vital that players are aware of where a counter-attack is likely to initiate from and fill that area as quickly as possible. In the main, regardless of where the ball is lost, a counter-attack will be most successful if it is allowed to emanate from the central area in front of your defense. The first 6 seconds after losing the ball are the most dangerous for your team and the importance of gaining your compact defensive shape behind the ball as quickly as possible is paramount. Steps should be taken to identify the fulcrums of the counter-attack and mark them tightly even when you are attacking, and also have a focus on slowing the game down immediately on losing the ball.

Actions such as filling the central area in front of the defense with at least 2 players will encourage the opposition play wide to the flanks which you will then find easier to slow down the attack. Once the ball is lost, immediately have the nearest man to the ball press aggressively to force the ball backwards, again slowing it down and also if this aggressive press leads to a foul, then again the game is slowed down for the restart enabling you to get back to your compact, defensive shape as a unit.

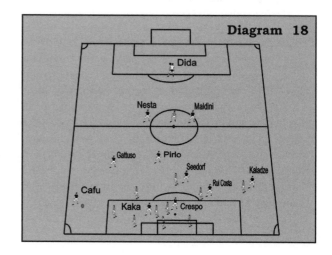

Out Of Possession and the Team Set

Whatever your defensive principles, this is the situation when you should be at your most resolute and difficult to break down. Forcing the opposition to play in a way that you want them to play should be addressed and having your transition players in half and half positions ready to counter when you win it.

Set Pieces

Quite simply, set pieces are responsible for over 1/3rd of all goals scored. Set pieces need to be worked on religiously during training in order to be successful with them. The 2 key areas of offensive set pieces are delivery and attitude to be on the end of the delivery. Whatever the practiced set piece is, the delivery must be constant into the target area and the players must be well drilled to attack that area and do so with conviction and belief. Defending set pieces requires organization and a commitment to get the first touch on the ball coming in, as this is a fundamental objective in reducing the amount of goals conceded.

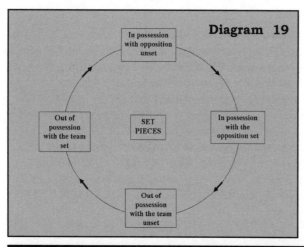

When devising the way you want your team to play, using the 5 pillars as the foundation of what you are trying to achieve will help a great deal in making your team a successful one. The complexity of all the different aspects and tactics involved within those pillars is for you to determine and organize, but a constant reference to them is essential.

David Platt

A cursory glance at the goals scored in the last four major tournaments, (World Cups 98 & 2002 and European Championships 2000 & 2004) show that over 40% were done so from set pieces. On average then, for every 10 goals scored, 4 are done so through a set piece or put another way, if 3 consecutive games had a result of 2-1 it is more than likely that one goal per game came from a set piece.

Looking solely at the last European Championships held in Portugal in 2004, 29 of the 77 goals scored in the tournament were from set pieces (33.8%). Of the remaining 48 goals which were scored in open play, 31 of them came from counter-attacks (64.5%). Added together, out of 77 goals scored, set pieces and counter-attacks were responsible for 60 of them (78%). As a coach, therefore, it is exceptionally important that a large time we devote on the practice ground with our players is dedicated to counter-attacking and set pieces, both from a defensive and offensive viewpoint.

Set Pieces

In my capacity as an Opposition Reporter for the English National Team during World Cup 2002 and Euro 2004, I had the job of filing a report on the teams I viewed. I saw over 15 games at each tournament and never saw any set piece which was over elaborate in its organization. Simple good delivery into the target area and a commitment of the players to attack that area yielded the most successful set pieces. Two examples of set pieces (corner & wide free kick) are given. Set Piece practicing can be boring for the players to undertake but it is essential to get them right in terms of delivery and commitment. The organization and detail of these set pieces can be done in a short space of time and then practiced with the aid of the session shown, which is enjoyable and yields both offensive and defensive organization.

Organization - Corner

Players are set up in positions for an attacking corner kick to be taken on attacking right hand side. The positions of the players for this corner make it difficult for the opposition to pick every player up and mark dangerous zones.

Coaching Points
- 4 attracts a defender thus making more space in the penalty area. He retreats to cover 3 who is 1 v 1 with the attacker before the corner is taken
- 2 attracts a marker again to create more space in the area. If no one comes near him he can receive and then cross the ball in
- 5 moves early towards the ball and then spins out to attack the back post, clearing an area where the ball is delivered. Anything over hit is his
- 10 moves towards the back post to attack anything knocked down
- 9 starts inside the goal where he is difficult to mark and then darts towards the near post when the ball is being delivered
- 11 & 6 attack the ball
- 8 rings the edge of the box

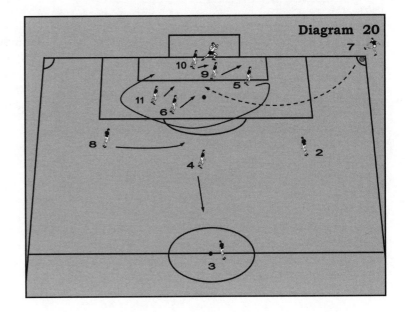

Diagram 20

Organization - Wide free Kicks

Players are set up in positions for a free kick to be taken in a wide position on the attacking right hand side. The free kicks are indirect in nature and are served into the penalty area to be attacked and scored.

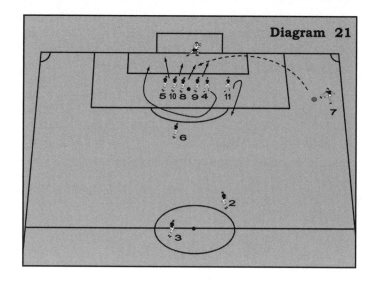

Diagram 21

Coaching Points

- 7 delivers to score in the back half of the goal inswinging
- 4 triggers the move off by spinning out to attack the back post if the ball is over hit
- 9, 8, 10 & 5 attack the areas shown
- 6 rings the penalty area
- 11 moves out to drag his man out of the hole to try to ease the passage of the ball
- 2 & 3 cover the lone attacker

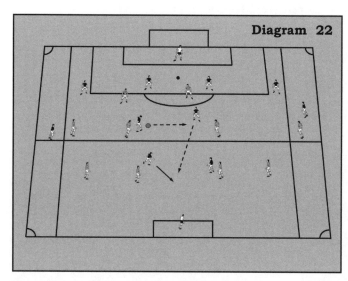

Diagram 22

Organization - Half Field Practice

Teams play 11 v 11 in a half sized field with a half line and two channels approximately six yards in from each touchline. The coach at various times in the game awards free kicks and corners within the channels, ensuring that the rehearsed set pieces are practiced and defended against.

Coaching Points

- All free kicks are indirect
- Players attack the ball with conviction
- Players must time runs accordingly
- Delivery must be accurate and well timed

David Platt

Organization - 6 v 4

In a 20 x 20-yard grid, four defending players play against six attacking players, four of which must stay on the outside of the square. When the defending team win the ball, they have three seconds to score a goal. Goals are scored by dribbling through designated goals or passing to a team-mate through designated goals.

Coaching Points

- Speed of play
- Move quickly to support ball carrier
- Attacking team to keep ball moving, move the defenders out of position

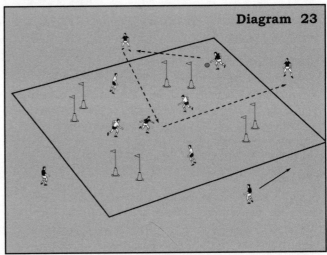

Diagram 23

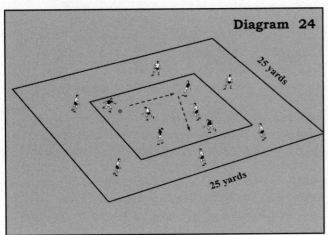

Diagram 24

Organization - Two Square Drill

Black team consisting of four players play against the white team of two players in a small 15 x 15-yard square within a 25 x 25-yard square. Once white team wins possession, they must play to one of their six supporting team-mates waiting in the larger square. The black team must regain possession and take ball back into smaller square to play 4 v 2 again.

Coaching Points

- Speed of play
- Move quickly to support ball carrier
- Pass and move to get open and change angle

David Platt - Tactics

Contributed by David Platt, former England National Team Captain and England U21 coach - now head of AFKUK at www.afkuk.co.uk.

Introduction

Whenever a coach is working on his defensive principles he will first look at the players he has at his disposal and their characteristics before deciding on where he adopts his first pressing line. Several player characteristics will determine where this press starts.

Forwards

Quick forwards such as Michael Owen, Ronaldo, Thierry Henry, etc. require space in behind the opposition which their explosive pace can exploit. This characteristic alone suggests that the team should defend deeper, allowing the opposition to come on to them so that the space is vacated behind them for when the team wins the ball. Forwards such as Raul, Del Piero and Ibrahimovic are exceptional technically and are at their best when they have the ball closer to the opposition's goal so a higher press suits them best, with the team winning the ball further forward which gives them the ideal opportunity to punish their opponents.

If however, this higher press is undertaken, it is important that the forward players are not lazy as they are easier to bypass by the defenders when they take up a more advanced position, especially as the back line of the team can come no further forward than the halfway line leading to a bigger expanse of space in between the back and front line of the team.

Defenders

Teams that have quick defenders such as Manchester United with Ferdinand and Silvestre and Arsenal with Campbell and Toure, can defend high up the pitch as the space they leave behind them is less dangerous due to their pace making them favorites to get to any ball played over and behind them. Teams such as Liverpool however, with Carragher and Hyppia are less likely to defend high due to their relative lack of pace and thus will take up deeper positions, making the forwards come back as well so they can retain their compact unit.

Midfielders

The midfield and the combative qualities of the players who make it up would also be a factor as it is this area where the majority of balls are won back from the opposition and counter attacks are initiated from.

Changes to the game

Rule changes to the offside law over the last few years have led to coaches readdressing their strategies. Furthermore, players are fitter and quicker than they ever where, more technically gifted and agile and very adept at taking only one touch of the ball before releasing a dangerous penetrative press. A forward who plays on the shoulder of the last defender only has to be level as the ball is played and he is deemed onside which has led to the top teams defending deeper, as once a back four is in place with no space behind it, with players in front of this unit forming a second barrier, it is very difficult for any team to break down. This factor alone has led coaches to imagine that the best form of defending is to drop off and invite the opposition on to them in order to maintain a compact unit from which to start to defend.

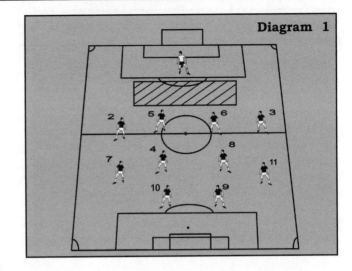

Diagram 1

In this diagram, we can see the general arrangement of a team that presses high and the weak area behind the back line that this causes.

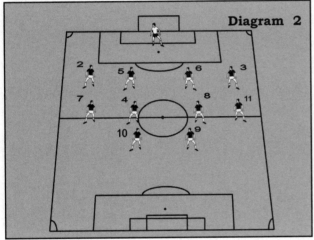

Diagram 2

In this diagram, we show a deeper press where the team has dropped off. This example is clearly more resolute, yet many teams want to play the game at a high tempo and this lack of pressure on the ball can often slow down the tempo of the game. Furthermore, a team that is chasing the game or feels it has superior players may wish to press higher and dominate the opposition. Traditionally it has been taught that in order to defend as a unit there must be a compact nature of the team, with a distance from front to back of approximately 35-40 yards at most. Both these diagrams show this traditional compact nature.

There is a shift however towards a more cavalier approach and I have seen both Portugal (Euro 2004) and AC Milan (Champions League 2005) press very high as a team, chasing every ball and closing down the opposition all over the pitch, while at the same time defending relatively deep to negate the space behind the back line. This requires a more unsymmetrical shape about the team and a definitive pressure to force the ball, and the player in possession, to play in the manner which the defending team wants them to. Both teams start high up the pitch and begin to press in earnest when the ball goes wide.

In this diagram, we see Portugal's defensive set up to press when the ball is with the left fullback of the opposition. The front three players, (Figo, Ronaldo & Pauleta) are involved in the first pressure to win the ball and are supported by Deco. They are supported from a deeper position by Maniche with Costinha, ostensibly defending along with the two centre halves and the opposite fullback to the ball. Note the depth of the back two central defenders who remain disattached from the rest of the team, with the opposite fullback strengthening this unit of two with his covering position. If this first press is broken, then there is an immediate retreat of the back four, along with Costinha and Maniche who foregoes his supportive role of the front players to help out those at the back, making a defensive block of six.

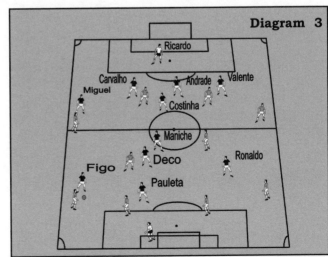

Diagram 3

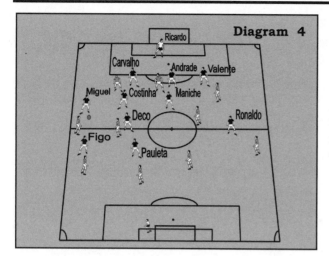

In this diagram, the forward players then file back to take up positions from which they can help out defensively if needed, though primarily as fulcrums for the counter attack, especially Deco.

Milan operate in a similar fashion as shown here. Their formation of 4-3-2-1 will, in the main, retain its shape whether in attacking or defending mode. Again, note the depth of the team defensively which conflicts with the high nature of the initial press. Both Portugal and Milan are stretching the 'rules' of defending and are doing so in a very successful manner. Could we be seeing a major shift in the game in the making?

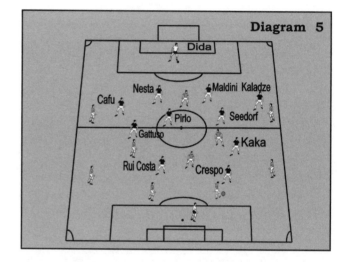

Sheffield United Academy

These sessions, observed at the Sheffield United Academy by Ozzie White, are from our recent trip over to the UK. Sam Saif conducted the session with the U15's, Scott Sellars conducted the session with the U17's and Ron Reed worked with the U19's. All three teams did the same warm-up, which was conducted by Kevin Paxton. The main theme of the sessions was passing and controlling.

Warm-Up

Four cones are placed in a diamond formation. Players line up behind two of the cones. Players then jog and perform different movements to the opposite cone, then back to the starting cone.

Coaching Points

- Heel kicks
- High knees
- Groins in
- Groins out
- Knee up and out
- Side to side

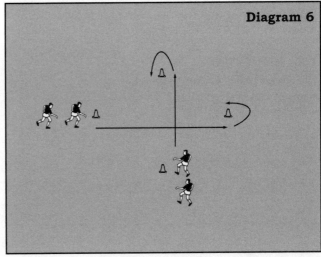
Diagram 6

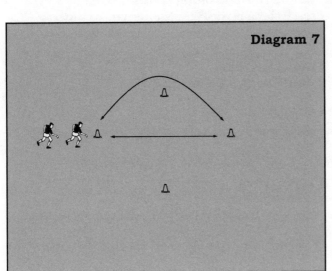
Diagram 7

Warm-Up (Continued)

Players continue to work in the same set up as previous exercise.

Coaching Points

- Four times - backward and forward then around
- Four times - sideways, then around

Warm-Up (Continued)

Players line up behind one cone and follow a specific pattern.

Coaching Points

- 1 - Backwards
- 2 - Open body shape
- 3 - Sprint to end cone

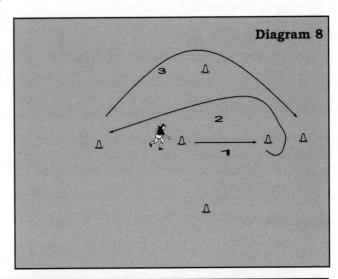
Diagram 8

U15 Session

Passing & Controlling

Two players work at opposite ends of a 15 x 10-yard grid. Player one passes to player two who controls and moves the ball away to return back to player one.

Coaching Points

- Good accurate, weighted passing
- Be on toes ready to control
- Soft first touch

Progressions

- Work right and left foot
- Repeat so both players work on passing and controlling

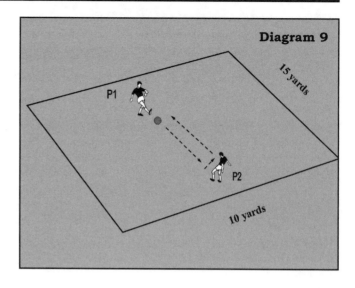

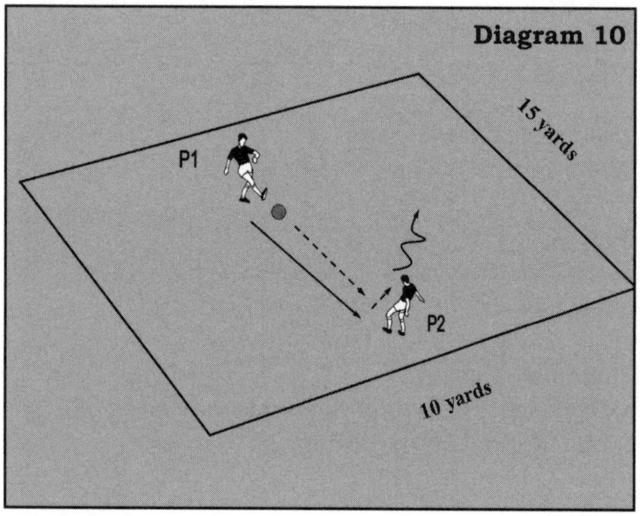

Diagram 9

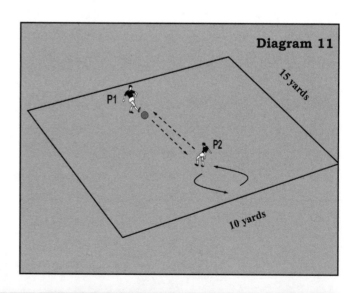

Diagram 10

Passing & Controlling (continued)

Same set up as previous exercise. Player one passes to player two and follows pass to close down player two.

Coaching Points

- Good accurate, weighted passing
- Be on toes ready to control
- Soft first touch
- Head up to see oncoming pressure - control ball away from the danger

Progressions

- Work right and left foot
- Repeat so both players work on passing and controlling

Passing & Controlling (continued)

Same set up as previous exercise. Player one passes to player two. Player two receives and then plays back to player one, spins out and then checks back in to receive the next pass.

Coaching Points

- Good accurate, weighted passing
- Be on toes ready to control
- Soft first touch
- Spin away to create space and then check in fast and call out for the ball

Progressions

- Work both feet
- Repeat in both directions

Diagram 11

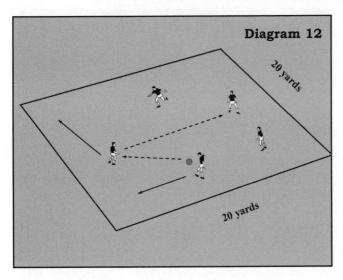

Diagram 12

20 yards

20 yards

Passing & Moving

Within a 20 x 20-yard grid, players are split into groups of five with one ball per group. Players pass amongst themselves moving in and around the grid.

Coaching Points

- Good accurate, weighted passing
- Be on toes ready to control
- Soft first touch

Progressions

- One-touch passing only
- Introduce another ball

Passing & Moving 5 v 5 v 5

Three 20 x 20-yard grids with five players in each grid. Group one plays keep-away until the ball can be passed to group three. The middle group sends in two defenders into the grid where the ball is. The remaining three defenders try to intercept the pass from one grid to the other.

Coaching Points

- Pass and move to create new passing angles
- Move defenders around to create space

Progression

- Rotate groups

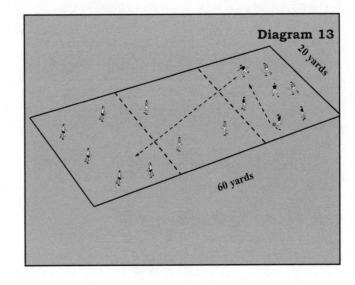

Diagram 13

20 yards

60 yards

Diagram 14

Crossing & Shooting

Players are split into four groups. Two groups act as servers and line up by each goal post. The other two groups line up diagonally opposite, approximately 15-18 yards out and act as attackers. The servers take turns to cross for attackers to head or volley on goal.

Coaching Points

- Accurate delivery allowing shot on target
- Head over ball when shooting - keep volley on target
- Be positive when shooting - aim for corners

Progression

- After serving - follow pass and switch groups

Sheffield United Academy

U17 Session

Keep-Away

Players form a circle with two defending players in the middle. Outside players try to maintain possession by passing to each other while middle defenders try to intercept or tackle.

Coaching Points

- Be on toes ready to receive and pass
- Defenders must work hard and anticipate

Progressions

- One touch only
- Must have two touches
- Must have three touches

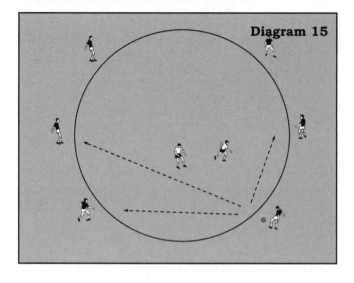

Diagram 15

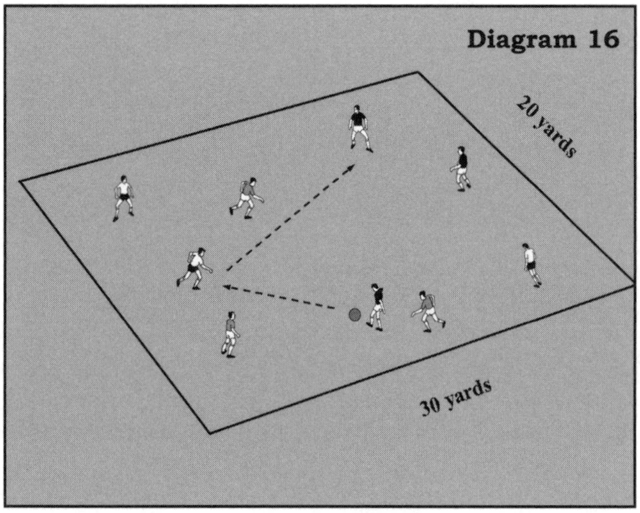

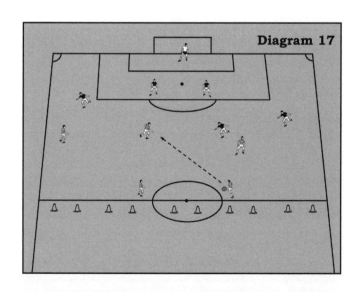

Diagram 16
20 yards
30 yards

3 v 3 v 3 Possession

Within a 30 x 20-yard grid, players are split into three groups of three. Two teams combine to play against the third team. The defending team must intercept the ball or force it out of the grid. The team that turns over possession becomes the defending team.

Coaching Points

- Keep the ball to set up the switch
- Accurate passes

Progression

- Restrict touches on the ball

Half Field Practice 5 v 5

Using one half a regular sized field, one large goal is placed at one end with five mini goals placed on the half way line. Five players attack the mini goals and must dribble the ball through to score a goal. Five players defend the mini goals and must attack the normal goal

Coaching Points

- Defenders defending the mini goals must defend as a unit
- Apply pressure
- Make play predictable
- Provide pressure, cover, balance
- Move together when ball moves

Progression

Diagram 17

Rangers F.C. Academy

Contributed by Mike Saif. I saw parts of this U12 session while observing a Rangers U11 session. It caught my attention for two reasons. First, the players were having a blast and loving every minute of this small-sided game, and second, no matter how much I observed, I couldn't quite figure out exactly what the rules of the game were. Fortunately, I was able to visit with coach Ian Currie after the session who was kind enough to explain everything. Currie is actually a scout for the Rangers Academy but was filling in for this session as the regular U12 coach wasn't available. Currie called it the "Four Goal Game". He said it was used regularly at Chelsea since Mourhino became the manager.

Four Goal Game

Place four small goals with goalkeepers on a 40 x 40-yard field. Organize four teams of three, with each team in a different color jersey. Each team is designated a goal to defend.

The objective is for the teams to play with each other (they can pass to any player from theirs or any other team) and attempt to score in any goal except the one they are defending.

When a team concedes a goal, they have to take a player off the field and play with just two players. Once another goal is scored, the player is allowed back on the field and replaced by a player from the team that has just conceded the goal.

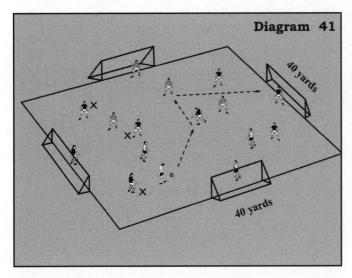

Diagram 41

Coaching Points

- Don't lose possession near your own goal
- Look for longer passes away from your goal
- Change direction
- Shoot early and often

Observations

- The players absolutely loved this game and played with incredible enthusiasm
- There was lots of communication
- As the session progressed, more shots were taken

Golden Goal

This goal was scored by Michael Owen for Liverpool against Tranmere Rovers in a fourth round F.A. Cup tie in 2001. This goal is a good example of playing an accurate, EARLY long pass (not a hopeful kick) to expose the opponent's defenders. Only the players involved are shown so as not to clutter the diagrams.

Liverpool have possession in their own half and pass the ball inside from the right fullback to the center defender, Sammy Hyypia. Hyypia glances upfield before he receives the ball and then plays a long 50-yard pass to the running wide midfielder, Danny Murphy.

NOTE: Murphy had started his run before Hyypia had received the ball, which gave Hyypia the target to aim for.

Murphy, got past his marker and controlled the ball perfectly.

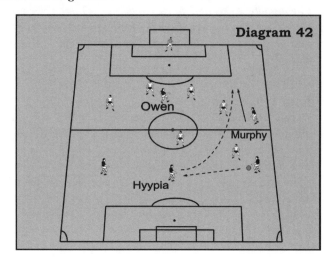

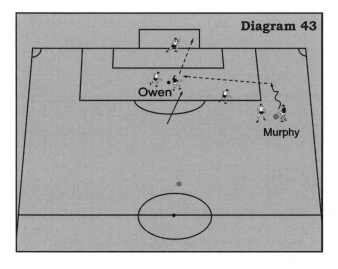

With a great first controlling touch out of his feet, Murphy was able to attack the end line with his marker chasing him.

As Murphy receives the ball, Owen makes his forward run and finds the space between two defenders.

Murphy slides the ball across to Owen just before the approaching defender reached him and Owen side-footed the ball into the corner, giving the goalkeeper no chance.

From the ball being played to Hyypia, the goal took about five seconds and just two passes.

David Platt - Tactics

Contributed by David Platt, former England U21 National Team Coach and now head of AFKUK.

The 2005 Champions League winners, AC Milan, have a philosophy to press the ball in all areas of the pitch, forcing the opposition play at a very quick tempo. If Milan loses possession, the closest player to the ball will press immediately with the other players aiding him as the team shape rarely gets out of position. The only problem area for Milan is on the flanks as the fullbacks are very offensive minded, though midfielders Gattuso and Seedorf cover this area if they are not involved in the attack. They operate defensively in three phases.

Phase One
When the ball is in the opposition defensive third, Milan shape up to force the ball into wide positions and from there, close down very aggressively. ATTACKING PRESS

Phase Two
If the opposition can switch the ball, then they work extremely hard at getting across the field to meet the opposition as high up the field as they possibly can. How high they can press the opposition is decided by the outside central midfielder, who will either get across horizontally or forward diagonally dependent on the pass and how advanced the player receiving the ball is. The rest of the team slide across accordingly. It is apparent that the distance between this high press and the back line does not stay compact, with the back line defending deeper than it would do conventionally. MIDFIELD PRESS

Phase Three
Should the opposition break through this midfield press, then the whole team drops deeper to defend the edge of the penalty area. The "hole" players will file back to fill spaces but they are ready to counter-attack quickly, with the CF also filing back to effect the same tactic. Compactness of the team comes more from front to back than back to front. DEFENSIVE PRESS

Offensively, the players are all comfortable on the ball. They will look to counter-attack as soon as they win the ball but if they have to build up with patient passing, they are more than capable of doing so. The fullbacks push up into the opponents half and the center halves are happy to spread very wide and progress with the ball if needed. The two players who operate in the hole, create problems for the opposition midfielders and defenders as to who picks them up.

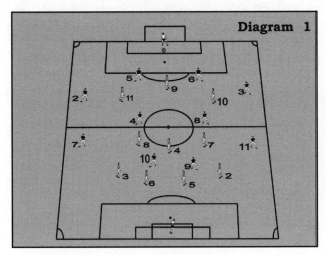

The 4-3-2-1 would set up as shown to invite the ball to be played out from the back.

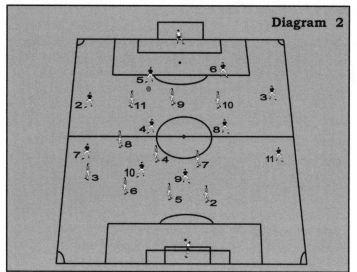

Players move accordingly to invite the ball out to black 2. Black 5 does have an option to switch to Black 3 in one pass, which would then trigger off the diagonal press through gray 7 & 10, as seen later.

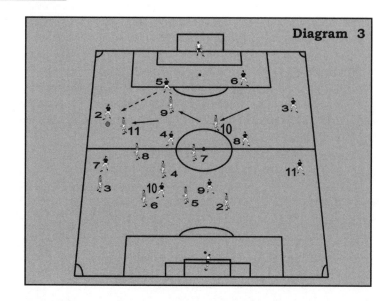

Once black 2 gets the ball, gray 11 presses aggressively, showing outside. Gray 9 closes off the pass back to 5, gray 10 gets in a good counter-attack position. Gray 4 screens and gray 8 is also ready for the counter-attack but ready to stop the ball if passed inside.

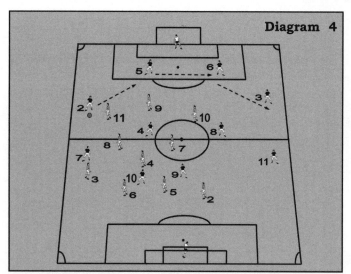

If a switch is effected slowly through the back four, then this enables the shape to be retained and the attacking press is still possible....

David Platt - Tactics

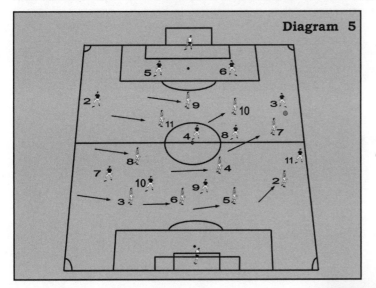

Diagram 5

..... The team has to work very hard to get across quickly and keep the black team under pressure.

If the black team can switch the ball quickly, then this would trigger off the midfield press as gray 7 would realize that the team cannot get across quickly enough.

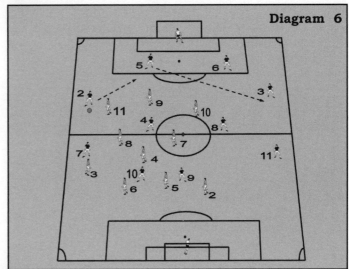

Diagram 6

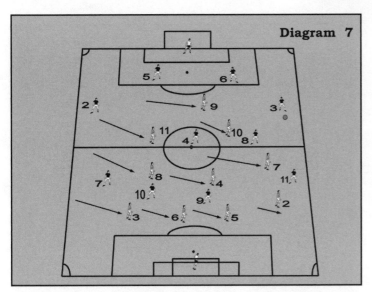

Diagram 7

So the press would happen in the midfield area and the recovery runs would be backwards of square from the whole team, respecting the fact that the black team have some time on the ball. Once set back into shape, the press would come forward again. At this point it is worth noting that the back four defends relatively deep compared to the rest of the press, aware that the space behind them is a danger.

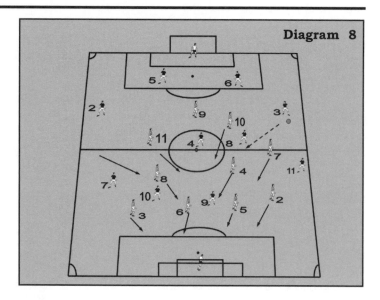

If the black team manages to pass inside and get the ball into a central position, the danger would be respected and recognized. The whole team would drop off with the back four hitting the edge of the penalty area and then staying there, with the midfield backing up close to them. The two split strikers, gray 10 & 11, would be fulcrums for a counter attack but in positions to defend their area with the lone striker as high as possible.

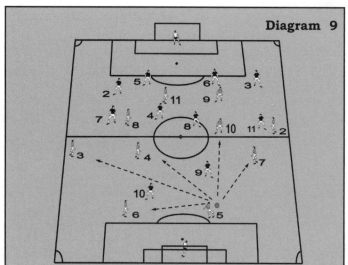

The key to the offensive creativity is to push the fullbacks (gray 2 & 3) up into the opposition half to ensure that space is created for gray 4. Gray 5's options on the ball are shown.

If gray 4 can get on the ball, then it is vital that gray 9 looks in behind to create the space for gray 10 & 11 to receive and turn. Gray 4's other options are shown as the black team cannot take care of all the offensive players and cover their teammates.

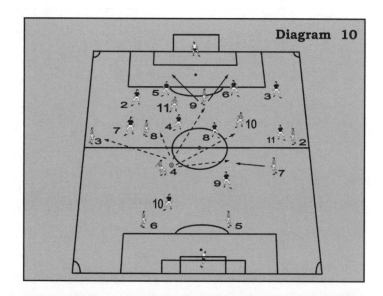

David Platt - Tactics

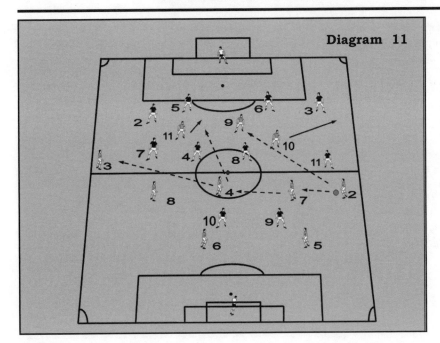

Diagram 11

If either gray 2 or gray 3 receive the ball in the middle or defending third, gray 10 or 11 must provide width, so as to create the space in the center for other players to receive and for gray 4 to have time and space to receive and play. Gray 4 plays like a quarterback.

If play breaks down, the two center halves and the three central midfielders form the central block that negates the counter-attack.

Celtic Youth Academy

The following are exercises undertaken at the Celtic Youth Academy with various age groups from U12 - U19. The drills were conducted by Academy Director Tommy Burns and Academy coaches Danny McGrain and Willie McStay. Burns is now the coach of the Celtic First Team.

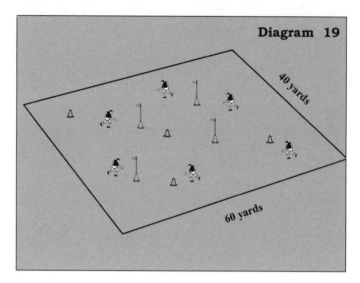

High Intensity Warm-Up

Players complete four different running activities within a 60 x 40-yard grid. They perform for four minutes and then have a three-minute break in between activities. Players run around cones, hurdles and dummies.

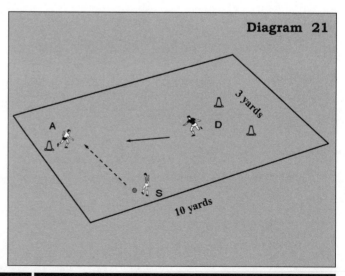

4 v 4

Two teams of four play within a 30 x 20-yard field with goals at each end. The game is played at a very high intensity with extra balls placed around the perimeter to keep the game going.

Progressions
• Rotate positions
• Restrict touches on the ball

1 v 1

The attacker (A) must dribble the ball through a set of cones three yards apart and 10 yards away. The defender (D) must prevent A from scoring. The server (S) passes into the forward for the exercise to start. Player A must make different runs to receive.

Coaching Points
• Overlap coach
• Go to defender, then check to ball
• Angled run toward coach

Progression
Rotate positions

Celtic Youth Academy

1 v 1 To Goal

Using a similar set up as before, now the attacker must attack a large goal protected by a goalkeeper. The defender lines up by the side of one post and passes the ball to the attacker who is waiting at the edge of the area. The defender follows pass to pressure the attacker. The attacker must control the ball first before shooting.

Coaching Points
- Receive at speed
- First touch away from pressure
- Can you shoot early?

Progression
Rotate positions

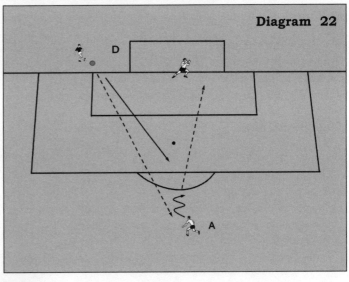

Diagram 22

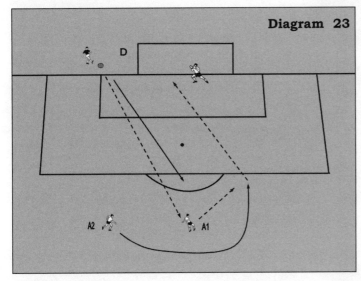

Diagram 23

1 v 1 + 1 To Goal

Same set up as earlier, defender plays out to attacker 1. Attacker 2 now provides support and both attackers try to score.

Coaching Points
- Support player
  - Overlap
  - One/two
  - Takeover
  - Become target player

Progressions
- Rotate positions
- Play offside

3 v 2 Fast Attack

Three attackers combine to score past two defenders and a goalkeeper. The attackers start with the ball, 25 yards from goal. The attackers have 15 seconds to score.

Coaching Points
- Attacking players
  - Overlap
  - Decision making
  - Combinations
  - Speed of play
- Defending players
  - Slow the play down - delay

Progressions
- Rotate positions
- Play offside

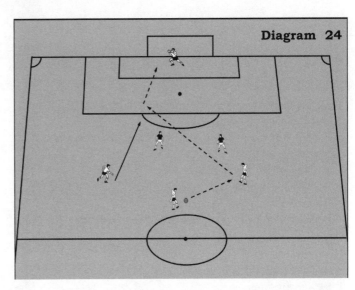

Diagram 24

Celtic Youth Academy

3 v 3 + Target Player

Teams play 3 v 3 in a 20 x 20-yard grid. Each team has a target player in an "end zone" at each end of the grid. Teams play keep-away for eight three-minute games.

Coaching Points
- Keep ball
- Change direction
- Unbalance defense
- Only use target players when needed
- Target players receive, then drive into the grid and commit defenders (target player rotates with passer from the grid)

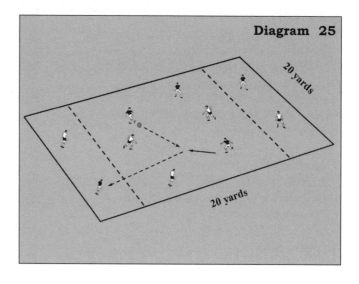

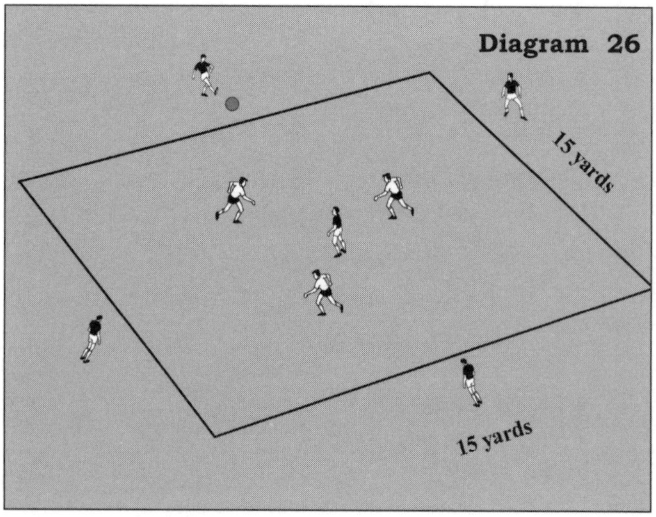

Diagram 25

20 yards

20 yards

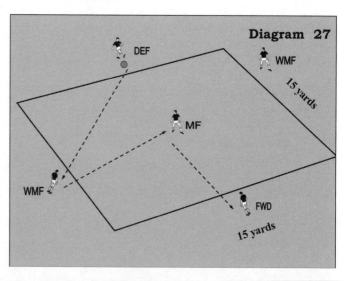

Diagram 26

15 yards

15 yards

4 + 1 v 3

Four attacking players on each side of a 15 x 15-yard grid, with another attacking player in the center. Three defenders pressure ball from inside of the grid. Attackers pass ball around and try to hit central teammate.

Coaching Points
- Body shape
- Disguise
- Decision making
- Pass selection
- Target players
  - Open up
  - One-touch
  - Body shape
  - Disguise
  - Awareness

4 + 1 v 3 Progression

Same set up as previous with defenders taken out. The drill is broken down to show how the grid transpires in a game positionally. Defender plays to wide midfielder. Wide midfielder plays into central midfielder. Central midfielder plays into forward.

Coaching Points
- Soft feet (suck defenders in)
- Body shape open
- Hit the front player - Penetrate
- Support - Midfielders constantly on the move

Progressions
- Bring defenders back into drill
- Rotate positions

Diagram 27

DEF

WMF

15 yards

MF

WMF

FWD

15 yards

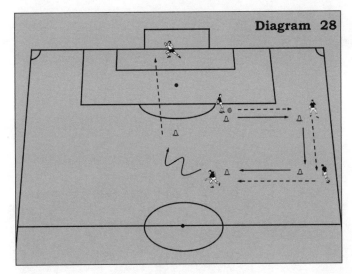

Diagram 28

Pass & Rotate

Four players make a square 20-yards out from goal. Player 1 passes to player 2 and follows pass. Player 2 passes to player 3 and follows. Player 3 passes to player 4 and follows. Player 4 controls and plays ball ahead. He follows the ball and shoots to goal.

Coaching Points

• Angle and timing of runs
• Bend shot around goalkeeper
• Fake the keeper with your eyes
• Follow up rebounds
• Work on weaker foot

Pass & Rotate Progression

Same set up as before. Player 2 now has choice - depending on the pass - to play around the corner to player 3 or to lay off to oncoming player 1. Player 3 has the same choice.

Coaching Points

• Receiver must check away first
• Angle and timing of runs
• Bend shot around goalkeeper
• Fake the keeper with your eyes
• Follow up rebounds
• Work on weaker foot

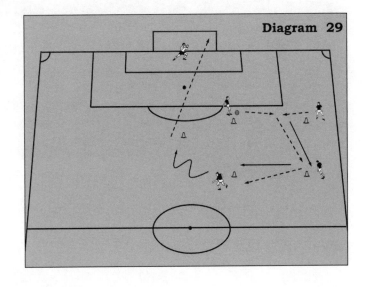

Diagram 29

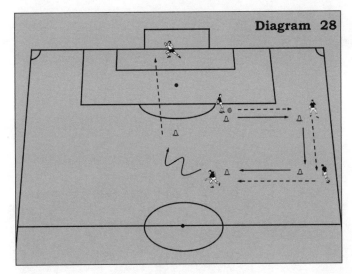

Diagram 30

Crossing & Finishing

Four defending dummies are spread across the top of the penalty area. Four attacking players are spread out. A line of attacking midfielders line up 40 yards from goal. Attacking midfielders plays into striker 1 who lays ball off for striker 2. Striker 2 plays ball out wide for wide attacking player, who runs onto pass and crosses for strikers and opposite attacking wide player to score.

Coaching Points

• Striker 1 must check away first
• Angle and timing of runs
• Accuracy of passing and crosses
• Strikers work on different combinations

DAVID PLATT BOOKS

How to Play Against and Beat the 4-4-2 including the 4-5-1 — By David Platt — $24.95

How to Play Against and Beat the 4-3-3 — $24.95

How to Play Against and Beat the 3-5-2 — By David Platt — $24.95

David Platt is well renowned as one of the world's finest tacticians. His playing career is unparalleled and gave him a great platform to enter the coaching ranks. Platt played in England with Aston Villa and Arsenal and in Italy with Juventus and Sampdoria. He also played 62 times (20 as captain) for the England National Team including the 1990 team that advanced to the semi finals of the World Cup.

As well as playing in England and Italy, Platt also coached in both countries with spells at Sampdoria, and Nottingham Forest. Platt also gained international experience when he was coach of the England U21 National Team from 2001 - 2004.

David Platt

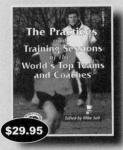

WORLD CLASS COACHING
Team Camps

Typical One-Week Training Schedule

Monday
9.00 Brazilian Warm-Up

9.25 Manchester United Shooting Drills

10.30 Juventus F.C. Small-Sided Shooting Game

11.30 Scrimmage

Tuesday
9.00 Arsenal Warm-Up

9.25 Ajax Passing and Possession Drills

10.25 PSV Eindhoven Possession Combinations

11.30 Boca Juniors Possession Scrimmage

Wednesday
9.00 Liverpool Fast-Feet Warm-Up

9.25 Manchester United Defending Drills

10.30 Juventus F.C. Defending As A Team

11.30 Dutch National Team Scrimmage

Thursday
9.00 Dutch Passing Warm-Up

9.25 West Ham United Breaking Out Of Defense

10.30 Brazilian Youth Team Playing Through Midfield

11.30 Brazilian Possession Scrimmage

Friday
9.00 U.S. National Team Warm-Up

9.25 Manchester United Crossing Drills

10.30 Leeds United Attacking Combinations

11.30 Scrimmage

Have Your Team Train Like The Pro's

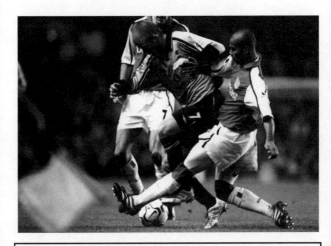

WORLD CLASS COACHING will design a one-week training program consisting of the same drills and exercises used by the world's top coaches and clubs.

We will then conduct those training sessions with your team for one week during the summer at your location giving you and your team an insight as to how the pro's train.

We will leave you with a team of players motivated to work and learn the things that made Van Nistlerooy, Beckham, Henry and Ronaldo into the world's top players.

Coaching Staff
Only top level coaches from professional clubs in England will be used to coach your team during the week long camp. Visit our web site for an updated list.

Cost and Availability
All camps will be arranged and tailored on an individual basis. Contact Mike Saif at 913-402-0030 or mikesaif@worldclasscoaching.com

Camp Options:
Camps are tailored to suit your team needs. Typical options are:

Morning 8.30 - 11.30am

Evening 5.30 - 8.30 pm

All Day 9.00 - 3.00 pm

Residential Camps

Motivate your players

Do the same shooting and finishing sessions as Thierry Henry and Arsenal.

Defend like Manchester United and Juventus.

Conduct the same possession practices as Ajax and PSV.

Learn the same attacking combinations used by Ronaldo and the Brazil National Team.

For more information Visit
worldclasscoaching.com